FIELD SPORTS LIBRARY

TOM FIRR OF THE QUORN

OTHER TITLES AVAILABLE

Famous Foxhunters
by Daphne Moore

Hounds of France
by George Johnson and Maria Ericson

Hounds in Old Days
by Sir Walter Gibley, revised by C. M. F. Scott

Way of the Gamekeeper
by Jill Mason

Gamekeeping and Shooting for Amateurs
by Guy N. Smith

Advanced Taxidermy
by P. A. O'Connor

For Denis Aldridge,
who kept Tom's memory fresh.

Figure 1 Tom Firr — Huntsman of the Quorn hounds

TOM FIRR
OF
THE QUORN
HUNTSMAN EXTRAORDINARY

by

ROY HERON

INTRODUCTION

by James Teacher, Joint Master of the Quorn 1975-83

Distributer:

Nimrod Book Services
(Fanciers Supplies Ltd)
Liss
Hampshire

ISBN 0 946474 281

Printed by:
UNWIN BROTHERS LIMITED
The Gresham Press, Old Woking, Surrey
A Member of the Martins Printing Group

Publisher:
Nimrod Book Services
(Fanciers Supplies Ltd)
Liss
Hampshire

CONTENTS

LIST OF ILLUSTRATIONS

INTRODUCTION

By James Teacher, Joint Master of the Quorn 1975-83

This is the biography of a great Victorian athlete — a national sporting celebrity — who brought honour to his profession, set new standards in the field and kennel and advanced the art of fox-hunting and the skill of riding to hounds. The legend he was in his lifetime still lingers on and it is particularly apt that on the hundredth anniversary of his and the Quorn's greatest season the tale of his life should be told.

Little is to be gained from jobbing back to the golden age of the chase. Momentary reflection reveals that not all changes have been for the worse. The horsebox and hound van have removed the grinding bore of long hacks to and from distant meets and have greatly added to the comfort of man and the working life of horse and hound. Modern veterinary science has contributed to the care, health and speedy recovery of injured animals. Refrigeration enables us to help farmers dispose of their dead stock and gives the hounds a consistent diet of flesh through the year. Many of the abhorred railways have fallen to the axe of Dr Beeching. The disused lines make convenient passageways through the countryside and provide refuge for wild life and cover for foxes.

On the debit side, the loss of countryside to urban sprawl, the incursion of motorways and the upgrading of lesser roads (the Fosse was not a practical possibility for cars and was completely overgrown north of Widmerpool until 1920) have reduced the amount of land available to hunt. Much of that has changed to arable and the accompanying agricultural practice has made the huntsman's job so much harder. Foxes seem more easily headed and are less able to make their point. Doubtless the number of cars and the speed at which car-followers can get about has much to do with this. During the last hundred years there has been an accelerating drift of people away from the land. The old farm cottages have been recolonized by urban commuters, some of whom have taken up the cause of nature conservation with an atavistic enthusiasm but occasionally fail to understand that field sports are an integral part of country life. Many conservationists grant the positive contribution the sport makes to the preservation of wildlife habitat. Firr would surely be astounded by the raging political furore and the time and money spent in attacking and defending the sport he so loved.

Since Tom Firr's day the Kennels have moved to Pawdy Cross-roads. This splendid Edwardian structure was completed three years after his death. Like all modern developments, at £14,000, it was double the estimated cost. The opening meet — still a most important occasion — no longer takes place on the first Monday in November but is more likely to be on the third Saturday in October. This has been brought about by the need to prolong the pre-Christmas hunting as the trend to early lambing, and the preparation for grass-keep sales at the end of March have curtailed our ability to continue into April. Shooting and hunting interests co-exist quite happily. The areas in which the Quorn will be hunting are made known in June and sportsmen cooperate in arranging their shooting days when we are unlikely to run their way.

The field, strictly controlled at less than half the size it was in its hey-day and sporting a higher percentage of the fair sex, still reflects a broad spectrum of society. The present Prince of Wales — great-great-grandson of the one who so admired Firr — is a popular and bold man to hounds. Famous horses and riders are to be seen galloping and jumping their way across Leicestershire. Masters are still bowled over by over-zealous followers: Mr Coupland by Fred Archer, myself more mundanely by the pop group *Showaddywaddy*'s drummer. Archer protested he had given the master 'at least a length and a half'. Quite a week for him: 'Four days hunting, five falls, knocked over two people and fined £1 and costs for riding on a footpath.' Out on the Monday following, a horse was killed under him. Not even Willie Carson carries his enthusiasm to quite such excess.

It is not out of place here to mention Michael Farrin, our current huntsman. He maintains the splendid Firr tradition, is an acknowledged master of his art and a beautiful horseman. He has been responsible for putting many young huntsmen on the right path. Lionel Salter (Duke of Buccleuch's), Chris Bowld (Blackmoor and Sparkford Vale) and Tony Wright (Exmoor), who incidentally continues the Firr vocal tradition, spring to mind. It would give Tom Firr the greatest satisfaction to know his pack is held in such worthy hands.

I greatly enjoyed my years with the Quorn and am delighted that the life of the greatest of its heroes should go on permanent record. What rides they had: what times we have. It has been, is, and will always be, the very best of fun.

James Teacher.

To Jimmy
with many thanks for the many splendid
days stalking we have had at

Figure 2   James Teacher (Joint Master) on *The Sheikh* with Michael Farrin (Huntsman) on *Dark Legend*.

Fealar
James Teacher

Michael Farrin

AUTHOR'S NOTE

At least seven authors have tried to write Tom Firr's biography in the last hundred years. The fact that I have succeeded is not due to any special quality on my part; more to changed circumstances, including the unstinted co-operation of Tom's family and not least the timely and generous intervention of James Teacher.

Otho Paget, who hunted with Firr, was one of the first to make the attempt but, like those who followed, he found unexpected obstacles and was not provided with the necessary material. In the 1950s there was a determined effort by Major Guy Paget, who believed due tribute should be paid to a man who was often described as the finest huntsman of all time. Guy Paget had a personal interest. He had been blooded by Firr at Barkby Holt; three of his cousins had been Masters of the Quorn and his son, Lord Paget of Northampton, was Master of the Pytchley for three seasons. Major Paget asked Colin Ellis, the Leicestershire author and poet, to collaborate in the project. Unfortunately, both men died before they could bring their plans to fruition. Major Paget was killed when he was thrown on to a road while out with the Fernie in March 1952.

A draft, unrevised typescript prepared by Guy Paget — with corrections appended by Colin Ellis — was sent to the present author through the kindness of Denis Aldridge, former secretary of the Quorn. That version became my starting point. Tom Firr's own brief and previously unpublished memoirs, in which he covers his early years, have been incorporated; and so have details from his hunting diaries, including the complete diary for 1883-84, to mark the centenary of *The Best Season on Record*.

I have received great assistance and many kindnesses from Tom's granddaughter, Grace Pickard, and her sister, Christine Greer, and I am indebted to them for making available material from the family archives. I extend my thanks to Lord Paget, who gave me consent to use his father's work, and to Michael Clayton, editor of *Horse and Hound*. I am also grateful for the help and encouragement received from Chloë Teacher, whose constructive suggestions improved the manuscript; Kathleen and Denis Aldridge, Lt. Col. Sir John Miller, Frank Osmond Martin, Ethel Ellis, Daphne Moore and from my family — Maureen, Ian and Sue.

While writing this biography I was reminded time and again of the influence which Tom Firr's career exerted upon the hunt servants who came after him, if only in setting a supreme example for them to emulate. In particular, comparisons were drawn between him and George Barker, a very different character but who did in fact better Firr's record of service. George was born at Thorpe Satchville, where he was tutored in the science of hunting by Otho Paget, and he went to the Quorn in 1922 as second whipper-in. He succeeded Walter Wilson as huntsman seven years later and he retired in 1959. Comparisons with the past are impossible to avoid. Three huntsmen, one in each century, stand out in the Quorn's history for their skill and length of service: Jack Raven in the 18th, Tom Firr in the 19th and George Barker in the present century. Now the Quorn have Michael Farrin, an admirable representative of the modern generation of hunt staff, who is well into his second decade as huntsman and seems set fair to challenge the records of his illustrious predecessors.

Figure 3 Tom Firr dressed for a wedding

Figure 4   Tom Firr — 1894, with his hounds (From a painting by John Beer)

COLOURED ILLUSTRATIONS

The coloured illustrations depict scenes from the Victorian era, a heyday for hunting, as well as Tom Firr and other characters.

Figure 1. Tom Firr from "Men of the Day" a *Vanity Fair* series.

Figure 2. Capt. "Doggie" Smith, one of the leading riders with the Quorn.

Figure 3. Otho Paget (Q) who hunted with Firr and who took over from Brooksby as correspondent for *The Field*.

Figure 4. *Quorn Alfred*, Tom Firr's pride and joy, and the cornerstone of his kennel. He was bred from in his second season, and by the time he was five, there were eight couple by him on the Quorndon benches. (Picture, courtesy: Daphne Moore)

Figure 5. Tom Firr on *Whitelegs* by Basil Nightingale.

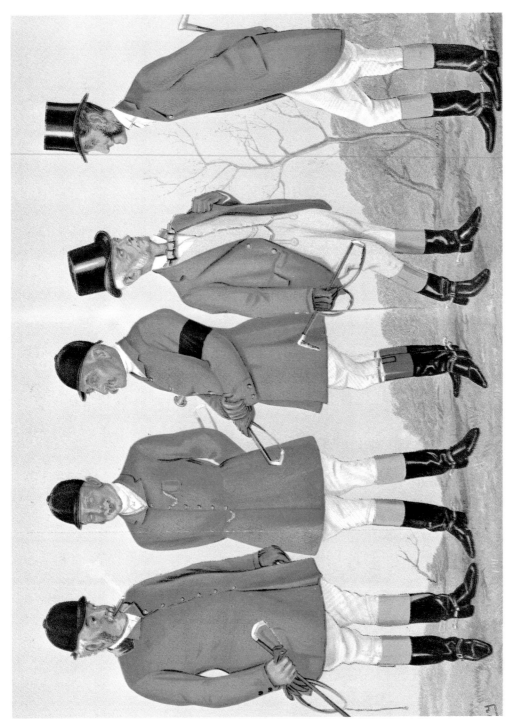

Figure 6. A Master's Meet from *Vanity Fair* in 1895 showing Lord Lonsdale (second from the left) with Captain Park-Yates (Cheshire), Lord Willoughby de Broke (Warwickshire), Mr T C Garth (Mr Garth's) and Lord Portman (Portman).

Figure 7. *Tom Firr with the Pack*, a large oil painting, artist unknown, from the collection of John Walker.

Figure 8. *The Quorn opening meet at Kirby Gate, 1901*, by Cuthbert Bradley. Tom Firr, retired huntsman, in the right foreground.

Capt. Whitmore
The Duke of Portland
Capt. Smith
Master Coupland

Master Burnaby
Sir Frederick Johnstone, Bar., M.P.
Capt. Middleton
Mrs. F. Sloane Stanley
Earl of Wilton
Miss Burnaby
Mrs. Coupland
Mr. R. W. Johnstone
Miss Livingstone
W. Little Gilmour, Esq.
Maj. Gen. E. S. Burnab
Viscount Downe Lord Manners
Sir Frederick Fowke, Bart.

Figures 5 & 6   The Quorn Hunt, Meet at Baggrave 1882

Boyce   Capt. E. P. Elmhirst   Ernest Chaplin, Esq.
    T. Turner Farley, Esq.   Countess of Wilton
                  Capt. The Hon. H. H. Molyneaux
                  Miss Webster

        Earl of Lanesborough
          William Chaplin, Esq.
  A. C. Barclay, Esq.   Julius Behrens, Esq.
Coupland, Esq.   Lady Grey de Wilton
   Tom Firr (Huntsman)

             Col. The Hon. H. Forester

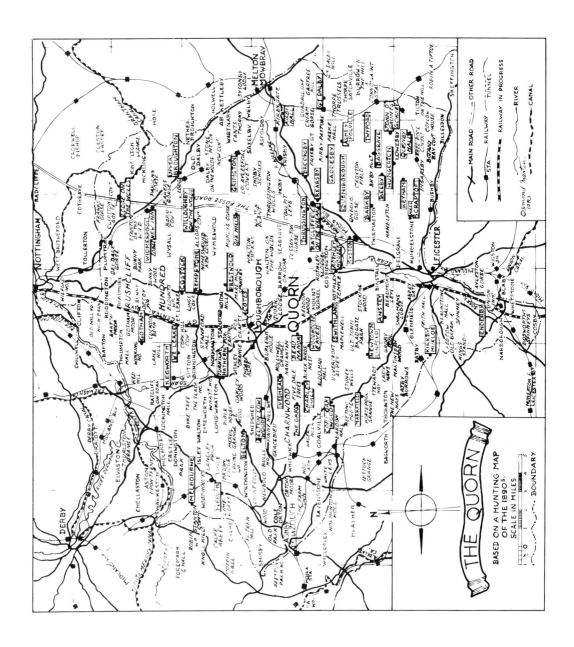

Figure 1.1   A Map of the Quorn

CHAPTER 1

THE GREATEST

Tom Firr's place in the annals of hunting has been compared to that of W. G. Grace in the history of cricket. Both men were innovators who stood head and shoulders above their contemporaries and they ushered new eras into their chosen sports. The standards set by Tom are as relevant today as when he evolved his marvellous technique. There lies the paradox. If by some time warp W. G. in all his glory were to be transported to present day Lord's or Melbourne he would be like a fish out of water. Yet one can imagine Firr taking his place at the head of today's Quorn field and, with a quiet word and an almost imperceptibe signal to hounds, moving off just as he did in his heyday.

Few men in any sport have achieved the pre-eminence enjoyed by Tom Firr during the twenty-seven years he hunted the Quorn hounds over the cream of the shires; the idol of princes and paupers and the admitted master of his craft, at the head of a field of hundreds that included some of the finest riders and amateur huntsmen in Europe.

Tom first tasted the joys of a racing-pace "burst" on the Leicestershire grasslands when he was a twenty-two years old second whipper-in. He did not rest until he returned as a fully-fledged huntsman with England's premier pack. And from that moment until his death his home was within earshot of his beloved hounds. He was perfect for the part in physique, training and temperament. He was also fortunate in the Masters and huntsmen he served and the types of country to which that service took him.

Who was the greatest huntsman? It is one of life's imponderables, for so much depends on the period, the setting, and even on the quality of the other Hunt servants and the Masters.

What can be stated with certainty is that, in his time and place, no-one else could have approached the perfection which Tom Firr brought to his work with the Quorn. In Tom's era fox-hunting was still evolving, fields were growing in size and the nature of those followers was changing from an exclusive circle of friends to vast numbers drawn from all strata of society. Towards the end of his career factories were closed for the day to allow workpeople to see Tom Firr and the Quorn, and he lived to experience the incursions of bicycle riders and the noisy, smelly debut of the motor car at meets.

Among Tom Firr's admirers was Brooksby (Captain Pennell-Elmhirst), the most respected of hunting correspondents, who said of him: "Under his masterly handling a fine pack was ever seen at its best; his method was so strong and exhilarating that it appealed alike to hounds, to sportsmen of mature experience, and to enthusiasts of whatever age. As Tom Firr's horn and scream brought hounds bounding out of covert a thrill would ram up one's very backbone. As he jammed the horn home — and invariably peeped at his watch — one knew that a gallop had begun and that joy was before us. While hunting a fox he seldom cared to have a whipper-in in attendance; his quiet 'yo-oi' was enough to swing hounds to their cast and to stay the most fervent galloper. As the pack went forward anew, so did Firr with a heart-stirring cheer of endorsement, and apparently with the easiest piece in the fence exactly opposite him. Other great huntsmen there have been, but only one Tom Firr — and he in the country and with the field most suited to him."

The attributes important to a huntsman are not only those which are seen in the course of a chase. Perhaps even more important is his unseen work at the kennels; the breeding and training of hounds, and the way he handles the staff. Not all those who arrive spick and span at a meet realise that the huntsman's day started before dawn and will not end until the sun has long gone down. In Tom Firr's period there were no horse boxes. Lord Lonsdale, late in Tom's career, sent a carriage for his huntsman, but that was an exceptional provision and for most of his hunting life Tom remained in saddle from the moment he left home in the morning to his return at night. If he had a cold, or if his troublesome back was painful, he could not cry off. He was Tom Firr and, come rain or shine, frost or snow, he had to turn out.

In the year of Tom's enforced retirement, Otho Paget, who succeeded Brooksby as hunting correspondent to *The Field*, wrote: "There are few men who do not begin to lose some of their nerve when they have passed forty; but, of course, there are exceptions, and the only huntsman I ever knew who retained his, riding to the end, was Tom Firr. At the age of fifty-eight, in his last season with the Quorn, he was riding to hounds in as brilliant a fashion as when he first joined the pack five-and-twenty years before.

"How much longer he would have continued to ride over Leicestershire, had he not met with the accident which laid him on the shelf, it is, of course, impossible to say.

"Future ages may produce huntsmen as good as Tom Firr, but we of his generation can never expect to see his equal. I consider he was as near perfection as it is possible to find anything in this world. He combined all those qualities which the ideal huntsman should possess. Hands, nerve, and seat made him a finished horseman. He sailed quietly over the biggest fences as if they were gaps, and he was such an excellent rider that you never noticed his riding. He was as quick as lightning, and yet never in a hurry. He had the patience to let hounds hunt out a cold scent, and knew the exact moment when to press them on to a beaten fox. His voice and hound language were perfect, and his cheer acted like a stimulant on the pack at the end of a hard day. Firr was a man who would probably have reached the top of the tree in any other walk of life, for he had more brain-power than is allotted to the average man. His mind grasped a situation at once, and action followed thought with the rapidity of lightning. He had a marvellous intuition of the way a fox had gone, and often recovered the line by a bold cast when everyone thought it hopeless. He trusted his hounds and was seldom disappointed. Such was the greatest huntsman of the century."

The second half of the 19th century saw the rise of many notable huntsmen, whose skill was said to be as great as any giants of the past. Will Dale (**Brocklesby and Duke of Beaufort's**); Frank Gillard (**Quorn and Belvoir**); Charles Payne (**Pytchley and Wynnstay**);

2

Figure 1.2   Frank Gillard

Thomas and Charles Leedham (**Meynell**); Will Goodall (**Pytchley**) and Frank Beers (**Grafton**) are among those whose names come to mind. A generation later came Arthur Thatcher (**Cottesmore and Fernie**) and Frank Freeman (**Pytchley**). And there are several in the modern era whose names would not be out of place in such company, although conditions in the last half-century have changed even more dramatically than in the generations of Firr and Freeman. Guy Paget espoused the claim of Frank Freeman to the title of "best ever," at the same time pointing out the impossibility of proving the point either way. "He was certainly the best huntsman of his time, though whether greater than Tom Firr will never be decided, for Firr gave up his horn six years before Frank carried one, so that few, if any, saw both men at their best." A parting shot in the argument can be left to the eminently sensible Jimmy Finch, who knew both huntsmen well: "I don't know which was the best, Firr or Frank, but I know the one I had most fun with, and that was dear old Arthur Thatcher, but he preferred to please his field than to kill his fox."

I'M GOING A-HUNTING

All the best huntsmen have been raised within sight and sound of horses and hounds. Tom Firr was born at the Essex Hunt Kennels, Copt Hall, at the northern tip of Epping Forest, on 12 April 1841. His birth certificate showed the family name as Fir, a usage they dropped soon afterwards. Henry John Conyers was then Master of the Essex; Jem Morgan was his huntsman (1833-48), Charles "Joe" Shepherd was first whipper-in and Tom's father was kennelman.

As a child Tom spent a good deal of his time in the kennels and stables and his first riding lessons were on a saddle balanced on a partition between two stalls, with a drop of six feet on either side. Tom's father, Abraham Firr, was an established hunt servant of long experience. He was probably of Hertfordshire stock, for his first recorded job was when he was fourteen years old, as a kennel boy at Puckeridge in 1814, twelve months before the Battle of Waterloo. Abe Firr was better educated than was usual for Hunt servants of his day. He could write a fair letter; he was ambitious for his sons, and Tom, the youngest son of a second marriage, had comparatively good schooling.

Abe spent a total of sixty-five years with two packs, the Puckeridge and the Essex. He and his wife, Susannah (née Brett), brought up Tom in the classic Victorian mould: upright, God-fearing and proud, with respect for the establishment, but with the strength of will to speak up against injustice. Tom was a true Victorian. Born in the fourth year of Victoria's reign, he died a year after the Queen.

Several authors have stated that Tom Firr had little education, and one well-known account maintains that he never went to school and that his wife taught him to read and write. In fact for eight or nine years he attended schools in the Epping area, when most of his generation left school at ten years of age. As Tom wrote in 1898: "Education in my day was not thought so much of as now, consequently I got but a very limited share of it, although I must freely confess I got quite as much of it as I wished for, at that time, for no fellow ever hated it more than I." His schooldays, he added, consisted of "six or seven years, with two more at a higher school to finish with. The latter school was kept by a Mr. Tuvetto, an excellent man in his line, no doubt, to whom I was to have gone by arrangement on a certain Monday morning in October." As it turned out, hounds were meeting nearby that day, and of the four Rs which Tom was studying, riding took precedence. His father gave him permission to postpone his entry to Mr. Tuvetto's school for a day.

"Strict instructions were given me to call as I rode through and to inform the master of my intention. Consequently, I rode up to the door, knocked with my whip-crop and asked to see Mr. Tuvetto. The gentleman came, I raised my cap with a polite, 'Good morning, sir, if you please, I have called to tell you I am not coming to school today — I'm going a'hunting. I will come to school tomorrow.' To my very last day I shall not forget the look that man gave me!"

The Master of the Essex, under whose mantle Tom learned the rudiments of the chase, was as colourful a character as ever rode a horse, hunted hounds or swore an oath at a recalcitrant kennel boy. Henry John Conyers was born in 1782 after his family had been settled in Essex for a century. He joined the Coldstream Guards in June 1798 as an ensign, received promotion to Lieutenant in December 1799 and "retired" in April 1806. A man grew up quickly in the Coldstream Guards. The drill sergeant who put the young Mr. Conyers through his paces told him: "Swear hat hem, sir, proper, or they'll think you har a bloody ninny, sir. Swear hat hem." Conyers was a willing pupil and no trooper could outmatch him in the range of his expletives, as the hunt servants found out when he took the Mastership of the Essex in the 1805-06 season. Shortage of money made him retire in 1808, but he returned. When he came into his inheritance on his father's death in 1818, Mr. Conyers accepted the full burden as Master, until his own death in 1853, spending more than £100,000 in the process.

Mr. Conyers's old age was childless and lonely, and with the years his weight increased until, towards the end, he had to follow on wheels. Tom Firr was fond of "the Squire," and there is little doubt the old man liked Abraham Firr's bright son, whose first lessons in the manners and customs of the hunting gentry were gained in Mr. Conyers's company. The Squire's death made a deep impression on Tom, who was then twelve years old. He had a vivid memory of a strange dirge from the hounds before most of the staff knew that Mr. Conyers had died. It was quite unlike the familiar "singing" of hounds in kennel. As Tom wrote: "The peculiar conduct of the hounds during the Squire's death is not, I think, generally known, and may not be credited by some. But, sleeping as I was in a room at the kennels, I am able to speak as to the facts of the case. At a certain time in the early morning hounds began howling in such a manner as I had never heard before or since.

"Each lodging house was provided with a bell, the pulls coming down to the bedside. A most excellent plan, although it is not adopted at any kennel that I am aware of at the present time. If hounds fight in the day and it is necessary to correct them, sometimes rather severely, a touch of the bell now and again while that correction is going on will be found to have a wonderful effect at night, when they happen to disagree and those in charge have no wish to be put to the trouble of dressing and going into the kennel for the purpose of restoring order.

"Upon the morning of the Squire's death, the bells were rung but without the slightest effect. So we went into the kennel, and as we succeeded in quieting one lot, and moved to the next, those behind started again. We were quite powerless to put a stop to the dreadful row, which continued until they left off of their own accord. Later in the morning, the news came of the Squire's death. As the hall was but two or three hundred yards from the kennels, hounds were plainly heard there. And at the very time when they were howling so dismally, their Master, the Squire, breathed his last."

The hounds were sold soon after Mr. Conyers's funeral. Abraham Firr, his wife and family moved back to the adjoining Puckeridge country, where Nicholas Parry was master. Abe's return to Hertfordshire and the kennels at Albury End was the final move of his career. He stayed there for another twenty years under Mr. Parry and for one season under Mr. Gosling, retiring in 1876, the year Mr. Gosling moved hounds to Manuden.

As his father was head feeder and his brother, Jack, became second whipper-in to the Puckeridge, Tom had plenty of work to do about the stables and kennels. He had learned to ride with the Essex. But his horsemanship and knowledge of hounds were polished in Hertfordshire. He also had an employer he could look up to, a strong man with an even temper who made his staff feel it was a privilege to do all he asked. Like Mr. Parry, Tom did not swear, even under great provocation.

From the Puckeridge kennels, Tom went on to occupy "two or three minor situations" — which included a year in Lord Macclesfield's employ at the South Oxfordshire kennels. He then went to George Hobson's Harriers at Buntingford, Hertfordshire, as whipper-in. Hobson's kennels were at Julian's Park, owned by the Maetkerke family from 1699. George Hobson's son was Fred Hobson, a prominent amateur steeplechase rider, who trained horses at West Mill, near Buntingford. Tom "had charge of the pack, the Master hunting them himself."

5

Figure 1.3   John Conyers with his Huntsman James Morgan

They were, according to Tom, an "exceedingly smart little lot, about twenty to twenty-one inches level, with rare necks and shoulders, which they could use, and were capable of racing a fox to his death in less than half an hour, as they fully proved." In fact Tom hunted and killed his first fox with Hobson's Harriers, an exploit that put him into hot water with Nicholas Parry, over whose territory the harriers ran. But Tom insisted that stories which angered Mr. Parry, about numbers of foxes being killed by the harriers, were untrue. "A brace of foxes was killed by the harriers that season, one of them when the Master was not out."

Tom went on: "Having drawn a turnip field for a hare without finding, we were leaving it when hounds struck a line — and away they went. The animal pursued had not been seen, and although we had our suspicions as to the nature of the beast, there was nothing to prove it. Hounds seemed to revel in the scent, and I do not think we could have stopped them, even if we had wished to do so. Twenty-five minutes of the best found them at a standstill in a covert near Baldock; they had entered the wood with a rush, but very soon their merry little tongues ceased, and all was quiet. Two or three came out with blood upon them, and this told a terrible tale. We were in difficulty and we hardly knew which was the best way out. We must either go into the covert, get hold of the animal and hide him away, or get off as quickly as possible after our legitimate game, the hare.

"We chose the latter course, hoping all would be well and that nothing would be heard of our morning's adventure. No such luck as this was in store for us. The incident was talked about, and when the earth-stopper went into the covert to stop his earths for the Puckeridge hounds the truth of the story was confirmed. The fox was found dead at the mouth of the earths, a convincing proof as to what had happened. Mr. Parry, of course, was still very annoyed and declared that we killed more foxes than hares!"

WHIPPER-IN

After a year with Mr. Hobson, Tom seized the first opportunity to get with foxhounds again and crossed the border to wear a red coat with the Cambridgeshire. The Master, Charles Barnett, of Scratton Park, Biggleswade, was then hunting with little support from his neighbours, who mostly preferred guns to horses. Tom became second whipper-in but he also acted as second horseman to John Press, an excellent huntsman whose son later whipped-in to Tom Firr with the North Warwickshire. Charles Barnett's father had died of fever while serving with the Scots Guards at Gibraltar, leaving him an orphan at the age of eight. At nineteen, while up at Cambridge, Charles had a pack of sorts and he later rode great distances to go out with the Oakley. He had a kindly disposition and a fine pack, but he did not have a bottomless purse. So he gave as little as possible for his horses and kept his staff to a minimum.

The Prince of Wales (Edward VII), while studying at Cambridge, was often to be seen riding with the Cambridgeshire. One day the prince was late and missed the first hunt, so Mr. Barnett drew again instead of, as he intended, going home early. At dinner that night the prince was told of the master's courteous gesture, and next day he rode over to thank Mr. Barnett personally, an example of royal manners which impressed Tom Firr.

When he had been with the Cambridgeshire for a short time, Tom began to look around for a post as a second whipper-in proper. He moved to the Craven, a heart-breaking country of rolling, flinty downs and sticky ploughs and boggy woods. Theobold

Theobold was the Master, Charles Berwick the huntsman, and the first whipper-in was Jack Firr, Tom's brother. Part of Tom's duty was to school fresh horses, for his natural ability as a horseman had already been noticed. Perhaps the best that could be said of his service with the Craven was that it taught him to be patient during the more unrewarding periods and in a most difficult country. He commented later: "The Craven is by no means a great hunting country, at least it was not at that time, and I should doubt if much improvement could be made in it. Very little sport was to be had there then, and I have since heard a gentleman say he had hunted in it for eight seasons and never saw a run the whole time. A sporting lot of farmers, but the soil was all against the pastime of fox-hunting. Hounds were, comparatively speaking, always unable to run for lack of scent."

At the end of the 1861-62 season Mr. Theobold gave up the Mastership and the hounds were sold to Lord Hastings, of the West Norfolk. Before the next season arrived James Coxe became Master of the Craven, with a fresh pack but without Tom Firr, who searched for another second whipper-in's place as soon as Mr. Theobold left. Tom did not have to look far. He was snapped up by old George Carter, huntsman to the neighbouring Tedworth Foxhounds, whose country lay partly in Wiltshire and partly in Hampshire. A dog-cart was all Tom needed to take himself and his belongings the eighteen miles to the Tedworth kennels.

George Carter had been huntsman to "Le Premier Chasseur d'Angleterre," as Napoleon dubbed Thomas Assheton Smith, founder of the Tedworth. The seal had been set on Assheton Smith's career by his eleven marvellous years as Master of the Quorn (1806-1817). A rich man, he hunted the Burton country for a time after his retirement from Leicestershire and then, in 1824, he started the Tedworth, gathering together a pack on the family estate and carving a new hunting country from a virtual wilderness. The establishment which Mr. Assheton Smith supported to hunt the Tedworth country was no less lavish than the one he had kept at Quorn. His death occurred four years before Tom Firr arrived at Tedworth, but the Quorn-based traditions of "only the best" were kept alive under the new Master, Lord Ailesbury, and George Carter. As a result, Tom was given superb horses to ride and had the joy of assisting one of the finest huntsmen of the day with a good pack, albeit in far from ideal country. He was shown the art of hustling a fox out of the tangled woods, and he learned more about the essential long-term aspects of hound breeding.

Tom Firr came of age with the Tedworth and his growing maturity is reflected in his notes about that season. He said of the much-admired huntsman: "Most hunting people have heard of old George Carter (father to young George Carter of Milton fame), a most excellent huntsman in a woodland country like the Tedworth, with the most remarkable voice I have ever heard. He was a very peculiar man, as I found soon after my arrival. Coming into the messroom about three o'clock in the afternoon, he said to me, 'Bring your whip, young man. We'll go and walk the hounds out.' I took my whip and went with him to the kennel door, which he opened, and out came the hounds with a rush, and most of them went across the park! Thinking it was not the proper thing to do, and that it was my duty as whipper-in to fetch them back, I halloa'd 'Back!' But it had no effect. "I was running my hardest after them when I heard Carter's voice from behind, shouting, 'Young man, young man, come here!' I went back to him, when he said, 'You may be a good runner, I won't dispute that, but you can't catch those hounds. However, if you stay here with me, you'll see they will come back. They'll come back when they are hungry, if

8

not afore.' Well, I certainly thought that very peculiar!"

Tom also recalled "rather a funny incident," which occurred when hounds were frightened by the crowds waiting to greet the Prince of Wales, who was visiting the Marquis of Ailesbury at Savernake. "The meet was held there," Tom wrote, "and as we waited with hounds about a quarter of a mile from the house, the many hundreds of foot-people formed an avenue, reaching from us to the house itself. When the house party appeared and mounted their horses, the cheering began and gradually came nearer and nearer, slowly but surely, as they rode along between the waiting lines of people. Hounds began to look around at each other, then up at Carter, their sterns going down at the same time, until fright grew to panic — and away they went!

"Photographers were there from Marlborough— although photography was quite in its infancy at the time — hoping to get a picture of His Royal Highness and the marquis among the hounds. But, unfortunately for them, their journey proved fruitless. Hounds had departed and at the time the meet should have taken place not one remained!

"Carter exclaimed in his peculiar way, 'Well, well, it's no good stopping here without any hounds,' and away he went, horn in hand, with the object of getting them together again, which eventually he succeeded in doing. But no meet, in the proper meaning of the word, ever took place." The day ended happily, however. "A fox was afterwards found, and quite a fair day's sport enjoyed."

★   ★   ★

FROM THE QUORN TO SCOTLAND

His brief association with the Tedworth was important to Tom's career, as it brought within his range a post with the Quorn. George Carter was sorry to see him go. The old huntsman must have thought highly of his young assistant, for he recommended Firr to Mr. S. W. Clowes, who had just taken the Quorn, in 1863, and was in need of a second whipper-in. Mr. Clowes had long been connected with the Hunt, having married a daughter of Sir Richard Sutton, former Master of the Quorn. Lord Stamford sold the pack to Mr. Clowes for £2,000, a large sum at that time. John Goddard was engaged as huntsman and the new Master kept on James MacBride, who had whipped in to John Treadwell, under Lord Stamford. The auguries were good, yet it was a far from satis-factory season from Tom's point of view. Obviously, he went to the Quorn with high hopes and what went wrong is a mystery.

There is no mention in Tom's writings of the reasons behind his departure after only one season, but it does not take a Sherlock Holmes to deduce that it was not a happy team he joined. Part of the blame can be attached to the acid tongue of MacBride, and Jack Goddard was not the most tolerant of men, whose temper was not improved by rheumatism. Tom remarked laconically that the Quorn was a different country in every respect to the Tedworth and he "looked upon it as a good move." One of his few criticisms of hunt staff — or anyone else — was reserved for MacBride, whom Firr was later to replace as huntsman to the Quorn. MacBride, as the first whipper-in, obviously had his eye on promotion, and at one fell swoop he had to contend with a change in the Mastership and newcomers as huntsman and second whipper-in. Jealousy probably soured the relationships, but, as Tom pointed out, MacBride did not make a successful

9

Figure 1.4   The Prince and Princess of Wales

huntsman when he reached that position.

An example of the exchanges between MacBride and Goddard was given by Tom. "However good a man may be, however persevering, however determined to do his best, there are times when the huntsman's wrath is incurred, and when words of the pleasantest nature are not always heard between them, especially one of John Goddard's temperament. I have heard some funny remarks passed from one to the other.

"Jim was rather droll, and frequently scored in his returns. Upon one occasion, when he had not turned hounds quite quickly enough, and Goddard was reprimanding him, Jim answered, 'I couldn't stop 'em.'

"'Couldn't stop 'em!' said Goddard. 'When I was a whipper-in I could stop 'em if they were within a yard of a fox's brush.'

"'Then I wouldn't give a _____ for a pack of hounds like them,' said Jim. And I was bound to think at the time that he had scored again."

Sport was generally poor in Mr. Clowes' first season. Only thirty-three brace were killed in eighty days. There was also a wave of protest about the increasing menace of wire in the Shires. Not that wire made much difference to Tom Firr's performance. He confirmed his reputation as a hard and skilful rider who, on second whipper-in's horses newly introduced to the country, was able to compete successfully with the best studs in the world. For instance, Julius Behrens had thirty-five horses standing at Melton, Westley Richards had thirty, John Coupland twenty-five, Lord Wilton twenty-five, Sir Frederick Johnstone twenty, Lord Calthorp sixteen, Stirling Crawford sixteen, Lord Royston sixteen, W. Little Gilmour ten and Major Paynter ten.

★   ★   ★

The end of the season saw Tom Firr on the move again. After his six years in bad hunting countries, it is difficult to imagine that any young man would leave the cream of Leicestershire of his own volition and go to a raw pack north of the border. But Tom's departure for Scotland was not so strange as it might appear from casual examination. The 14th Earl of Eglinton, who engaged him as second whipper-in to succeed John Wilson, was a well-known Meltonian and thus was well versed in the doings of the Quorn and its staff. He was the son of the instigator of the Eglinton Tournament and he had formed his own pack in a good-scenting part of Ayrshire on succeeding to the title in 1861, three years before Tom's appointment.

Lord Eglinton's determination in making a first class fox-hunting country in a part of Scotland overrun with roe-deer gained Firr's respect. It also provided a challenge, and Tom was not disappointed. On balance, he had a happy season, working under little George Cox, one of that great family of huntsmen, and John Ransom, the first whipper-in. Tom Firr's admiration for the earl's achievement is obvious from his account of that year. "As no hounds had been kept in Ayrshire for a great number of years," Tom wrote, "the earl had a very difficult task. For not only had every farmer and resident to be got into the ways of fox-hunting but other difficulties had to be overcome, as the fox had no existence there at that time and the coverts were full of roe-deer, the most tiresome of all riot that foxhounds can come in contact with. All these difficulties were overcome by his lordship, whose management of the whole business must have been extraordinary.

"Everyone in the country took kindly to the sport. Foxes were strictly preserved in

11

every part of it; roe-deer, by order of the covert owners, were shot and Ayrshire almost at once became an excellent hunting country — 'the Leicestershire of Scotland' as it has since been well termed. Not only were the aforesaid difficulties overcome, but so well did everyone fall in with his lordship's views that puppies were walked in the country the very first year; a puppy show followed (the first I ever saw, for puppy shows were hardly known then), and everything was put at once into good working order. Squires, the Lanark and Renfrew huntsman, was judge at the first puppy show, and had rather a difficult task in deciding as to the best of a very useful entry."

All was not plain sailing, however. Tom continued: "I have already mentioned something about the trouble roe-deer will give in a hunting country. Everything was done to clear them off, but of course it was impossible to do so at one stroke. Occasionally, one

or more would be found in the coverts, when the note of a hound or two would very quickly be heard — a convincing proof of their presence, for hounds might be as steady as possible among fallow deer yet perfect devils after the roe!

"*Dashaway*, *Duchess* and *Dauntless*, three black and tan descendants of the blood-hound which came from Mr. Baker's kennels of the North Warwickshire, were beyond cure. *Dashaway* in particular, for he would run on either side of one's horse to get after them. This innate love for the roe never seemed to leave them, although they could, and would, hunt a fox in excellent style as soon as one was on the move."

The hounds' instinct to hunt the roe was not surprising, since their bloodhound fore-bears had been specially bred to hunt deer in Lord Forester's Willey Park, Worcester-shire. Lord Curzon, when he took the Atherstone in 1859, bought a draft of the hounds and found them a success, but there were no roe-deer in Atherstone country.

Describing the Eglinton country, Firr said: "The greater part of Ayrshire is a country where fox-hunting may be carried on to good advantage. There is generally a fair scent, and it is surprising that such a country should have existed so long without hounds."

Tom's hard-riding methods appear not to have met with unqualified approval during his first weeks in Scotland. Lord Eglinton told him, "Your chief desire seems to be to gallop after foxes." Years later, Lord Lonsdale used the episode, and the lesson Firr learned from it, to support a criticism of Arthur Thatcher, the Cottesmore huntsman. In a 3,000-words letter to Thatcher, Lord Lonsdale pointed out that Lord Eglinton had told Tom he must change his ways, or go.

"On 26th December there was a very long run, and after hunting his fox for an hour and twenty minutes Firr went to a holloa, got on to a fresh line, hounds went away, and at seven o'clock in the evening fourteen couples of hounds were missing and they were eighteen miles from home. Lord Eglinton went up to Firr and said, 'Firr, how came you to overreach that horse like that?' Firr got off to look at the horse and said, 'He is not overreached, my lord.' Lord Eglinton said, 'Give me the horse a minute and look at this hind leg.' As soon as he had the reins in his hand he trotted straight home, leaving Firr to walk home and collect his hounds, saying, 'You have overreached your fox as well as your horse, for your horse is wellnigh cooked. Collect your hounds and walk home.'

"Firr has often told me that he suffered agonies during that walk home, but he collected seventeen couples of hounds before he got home." Lord Lonsdale also wrote that, after the incident, Firr "always did his best to stick to one fox, and that was the real making of him."

The Eglinton huntsman had no complaints, however. Referring to whippers-in turning hounds, George Cox said, "Tom Firr could put 'em into my pocket."

★   ★   ★

Figure 2.1   Colonel J. Anstruther Thomson

14

CHAPTER 2

THE WATERLOO RUN

A chance meeting with Colonel Jack Anstruther Thomson turned Tom Firr's career back to the Shires. Tom was anxious to advance to first whipper-in, an ambition which led him to travel south. He took the opportunity to visit Tattersall's, the Mecca of hunting men on a Sunday afternoon. There he ran into Colonel Anstruther Thomson — J.A.T. to the world of hunting — who already knew about Tom's skill and had a high opinion of the whipper-in's potential. After two seasons as Master of the Atherstone, J.A.T. had re-established the Fife Foxhounds in 1849, but the following year he took his hounds back to the Atherstone country. When Tom met him at Tattersall's J.A.T. had assumed the mantle of Master of the Pytchley, of which Brooksby wrote that a "bad horse cannot get over the country at all, and a second-class one will only spoil your pleasure and ruin your nerve." It took very little persuasion from J.A.T. to make Tom break off negotiations for a first whipper-in's job with the West Norfolk and accept second with the Pytchley — but with the wages of a first whipper-in.

J.A.T.'s pressing need for a good second whipper-in had been aggravated by the departure of his huntsman, Charles Payne, an old hand who had been with the Pytchley at Brixworth for sixteen years, serving six Masters. There was a clash of personalities, for the Scot in Colonel Anstruther Thomson made him careful of expenditure, although he could not be termed mean. Charles Payne, however, had been spoiled by free-spending Masters, under whom all sorts of perquisites had gone his way. Payne obtained a new situation with Sir Watkin Williams-Wynn.

With Payne gone, J.A.T. achieved his aim of hunting hounds himself, and he promoted to kennel huntsman Dick Roake, who knew the Pytchley country well. At that time the Woodland Pytchley had not been established and J.A.T. ranged over what is now two hunting countries. He sometimes had two packs out in one day, with Roake hunting the second, giving Tom Firr ample experience and making Tom's later elevation from second whipper-in to huntsman in a single bound a less spectacular jump than is often thought.

Tom said of the situation when he reported to the Pytchley: "Dick Roake was the first whipper-in and kennel huntsman at the time, and hunted the bitch pack during the first season, after which Colonel Thomson hunted both packs entirely. There was no additional pack at Brigstock then to hunt the North, or Woodland, part of the Pytchley country, but all was hunted from Brixworth.

"The Brigstock kennels were used for some three weeks at a time in the Spring and Autumn cub-hunting, and again after the season in the open country was over. During the season proper, the hound van with four horses, and Colonel Thomson as coachman, used to take us down about one day a week." The Pytchley country provided "any amount of good sport," recorded Tom, "everything being in excellent working order — a good pack of hounds, a capital stud of horses, plenty of healthy foxes, eighty-four and a half brace of which were killed during one season; and mange altogether unheard of!"

In Tom's second season with the Pytchley he took part in the Waterloo run, among the most famous in the annals of fox-hunting. The "great Waterloo" took place on Friday 2 February 1866, and it derived its name from the covert, Waterloo Gorse. Reports of the run brought to public attention the name of Tom Firr.

The meet was at Arthingworth. The Master noted that he rode *Valeria* and *Rainbow*; Dick Roake was on *Usurper*, Tom Firr on *Fresco*, and Charlie Anstruther Thomson, the Master's son, was on *Amulet*.

"I was staying at Sir Charles Isham's at Lamport, and hounds called for me as they passed," wrote J.A.T. "Rain had marred the early morning, clearing by 11 am and giving way to mild, still conditions, with not a very good scent in covert and a south-westerly wind." A fox in Loatland Wood occupied hounds for an hour and five minutes. They found again in Waterloo Gorse. "The fox lay so still, I drew all round the covert and back to the top before he moved," recalled J.A.T. "He lay among a heap of dead sticks. *Graceful* found him." And so began a run that lasted from 1.45 until darkness stopped them at 5.30 pm, just beyond Medbourne, with *Graceful* the last hound to hit off the line. "This was the best run I ever saw, and over the finest country and longest distances, straight," commented J.A.T. He later set out the salient facts, to answer heated arguments about the distances and times.

"The time from Waterloo to the earth at Keythorpe (where they may have changed, as Tom Firr saw another fox there) was one hour and fifty minutes. The total time was three hours and forty-five minutes; but we had a check, twenty or twenty-five minutes, at the windmill at Medbourne, and hunted slowly afterwards." Describing the early part of the run, he stated, "I take the distance to be: from Waterloo to Kelmarsh three miles; Kelmarsh to Keythorpe eighteen, as we ran it — twenty-one miles in one hour and fifty minutes. There were only four ploughed fields in that distance."

After all that, J.A.T. went to the Harborough Ball. When he had settled the hounds and horses at Brixworth, he got out a hack and galloped back to his host's home at Lamport; sat down to dinner at 10.50pm; got to the ball at 12.30 and stayed for two hours. "I was very little tired and was at Ashby St. Ledgers by twelve o'clock the next day."

J.A.T. had five mounts during the Waterloo Run. He said that Tom Firr's horse, *Fresco*, "carried him capitally up to Keythorpe, and there he stopped trying to get up to me when he viewed the fox." Tom left *Fresco* at the Bowden Inn for the night and travelled home on the box of the Master's carriage after the Harborough Ball.

The way in which Tom Firr handled *Fresco* is a tribute to his horsemanship. J.A.T. described *Fresco* as "a capital little chestnut (15.3 hands), which I bought from Dick Painter." He tried Dick Roake on him, but "*Fresco* would not jump a stick; he refused everything. I gave Dick my mare, *Valeria*, and took *Fresco* myself, but he was just as bad with me; would not jump and scrambled through everything.

"Next time he came out Tom Firr rode him. Galloping alongside of me, he called out, "I could win the Liverpool Steeplechase on this horse, sir.' After that no one else ever rode him and he carried Tom all the time I had the hounds and he rode him the Waterloo run."

Tom Firr's version of the day's events was contained in two poems. The first, and shorter, one is given here:

Waterloo Run

Tell me, old chap, if acquainted you've been
   Of the doings they had t'other day;
How the hounds ran away and beat them all clean,
   Every man who took part in the fray.
Waterloo was the place where they put up their fox,
   And away they all scuttled like mad,
Till one and another had settled their crocks,
   Each man looking darnation sad.
Round Kelmarsh and Clipstone, where many got spilt;
   Lorks bless ye, to me 'tis a wonder
Over Oxendon fields there was none on 'em kilt
   O'er the oxers which rattled like thunder.
Right on past Farndon and Bowden Inn,
   With many a stile that was broken,
Until but a few of the best were left in,
   Not one with much go could betoken.
When down to the brook below Langton they went,
   I seed there was sport, for none feared it.
They rode like the de'il — on being over was bent —
   Harry Custance was all though as cleared it.
Then on towards Cranoe and Keythorpe like crows,
   The pack skid away o'er the pastures;
How the folks follows arter, the Lord only knows,
   Each and all meeting many disasters.
Past Hallaton Thorns, where some cove got a view,
   "Yoiks for'ard," he shouts, "tally-ho,"
Till the Captain* came up, and his whistle he blew,
   "Come, tell me then, where did he go?"
"He's gone for the Welland, dead beat," cried the man;
   Like a genius, the Captain besought him.
Evening came on, and then darkness began —
   You bet, he'd like to have caught him.

*Colonel Anstruther Thomson.

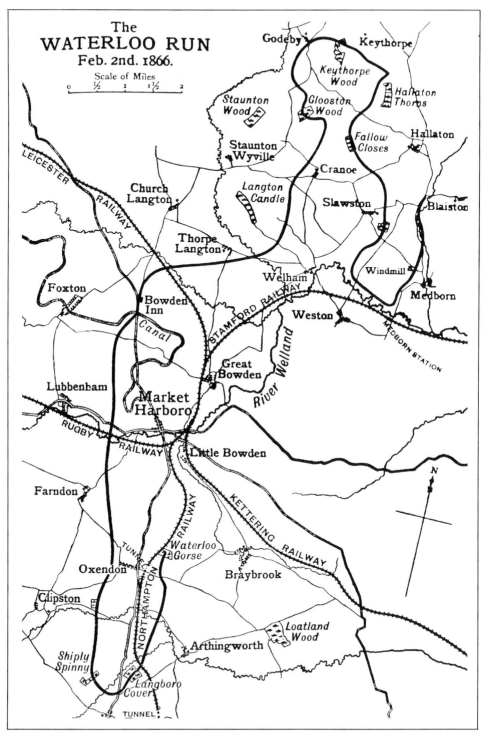

Figure 2.2   The Waterloo Run

FLYING WITH THE PYTCHLEY

No details of Tom's day to day life with the Pytchley were given in his diaries, not even of the serious outbreak of foot and mouth disease in 1865, when some of the farmers objected to hounds hunting over the infected land. There was no isolation zone in those days. The Cottesbrooke and Fawsley "doubles" became relics of the precautions taken to prevent the spread of the disease. Guy Paget commented in more recent times: "These are still formidable obstacles: an oxer, now generally wired to protect the ditch, a hedge, a bank ten feet wide; a hedge, a ditch and another oxer. Minus the oxers it is a debatable point whether it is better to fly or double them. Thomson doubled them; Frank Freeman plumped on flying, as one got over quicker and had a better chance to fall clear and could be up more rapidly. I expect Firr did the same."

Nor did Firr mention the distemper-ridden seventeen couple of hounds that arrived at Brixworth from the Burton kennels, some of them already dead. Payment was demanded for the hounds and J.A.T. seemed to have been more shocked by the request for cash than by the introduction of distemper to his kennels.

Perhaps more surprising was Tom's omission from his memoirs of his marriage to Mary Hannah Knight, the daughter of John and Charlotte Knight, of Northamptonshire, in 1867, after one of the Hunt's cottages was offered to them at Brixworth. But his mind when he was writing was on hunting, not family matters, as evidenced by his report of a run with the Pytchley that, while not as famous as the Waterloo, at least had its moments. It also had flashes of comedy. The other run happened "under rather peculiar circumstances and is quite worthy of mention," according to Tom.

"Huntsbury Hill was the rendezvous, the dog pack being intended for use that day. As was usual, Dick Roake and I were at the kennels to walk out and feed the rest hounds before going to breakfast ourselves and getting ready for hunting. A certain lodging house, which was generally used for the pack drawn for work on the day, for some reason had other hounds put into it, and the hunting hounds were put in another place.

"The kennelman usually got back from breakfast before us and went on feeding any hounds that were not in the hunting hounds' lodging house. Consequently, when Roake and I got back every hound in the kennel had been fed! Naturally Roake, who was in charge and responsible for any good or evil which might occur, was in a terrible state of mind. The only thing to be done was to send to the house and inform Colonel Thomson of what had happened. He quickly arrived on the scene and was, of course, very annoyed. He had to make the best of a bad job by drawing out about seventeen couple of those which had fed the lightest, making up a mixed pack, and giving us strict instructions not to mention a word of what had happened.

"It has often been said that a great many people who hunt pay little attention to hounds; that they do not know at the end of a day which pack has been out. Be that as it may, certainly no one suggested on the day in question that hounds had been fed — or that they even looked it.

"But to proceed with my story: the Huntsbury Hill covert lies hard by the meeting place and was always the first draw. We eagerly hoped that this would prove a blank, so as to give hounds a little more time to digest their food before the more serious part of the business began, but our hopes were quickly blighted.

Hounds had not long entered covert before first one spoke, then another, and another, and a good-looking fox was immediately afterwards holloa'd away. Hounds were out of covert without loss of time, and if they did not run together in their customary manner, or so that the proverbial sheet might cover them, at any rate they ran to the great satisfaction of a large field. From Huntsbury Hill to Saltsa Forest in the Oakley country was the run, and this was done, if not at racing speed, at a pace which was thoroughly enjoyable and the fox, a fine lengthy old gentleman, was killed handsomely at last."

No one admired J.A.T. more than Tom Firr. He said, "In a country like the Pytchley, where large fields come out regularly, there were sure to be riders good, bad and indifferent, and many who could hold their own over any country. Yet all must agree that not one amongst them could beat the Master, Colonel Thomson himself. Fences of all kinds came the same to him, and although I have heard it said that 'he crept through a country rather than over,' I am bound to say I have seen him do both. On a brown horse called *Fountain*, a flyer of the best type, I saw him clear Swinford brook in a style that put all others to shame, for not another got over near the place where hounds crossed!

"I remember crossing the same brook upon another occasion. A gentleman who hunted from London, I believe, keeping his horses at or near Rugby, came regularly on Wednesdays, and sometimes had another day or two in the week. His costume was peculiar, inasmuch as he always wore black kid gloves with a scarlet coat. Upon the occasion in question, he was riding at the brook about half a length in front of me, on my left, when, on reaching the water's edge, his horse swerved towards me and my horse, a real sharp one called *Fresco* (the very horse I rode in the Waterloo run), hit him in the shoulder and knocked him over into the brook in a most extraordinary manner, fairly turning him upside down!

"After the run was finished, and when drawing Shawell Wood for another fox, this gentleman came up to where I was standing at a corner of the covert, and sorry I was to see the plight he was in: wet, dirty, and a black eye. I thought to myself, 'It's odds he won't know it was I who upset him. I'll try him on the point.' So when he came up to me, I said, 'Hullo, sir, have you had a fall?'

"'Ya'as,' he replied, 'I-ah-cannoned with the whip!'

"'Dear me, I hope you are not hurt.'

"'Oh no, thank you, not at all,' he replied, an answer which showed that he did not belong to the faint-hearted division."

Of J.A.T.'s hunting method, Tom declared, "Colonel Thomson's style of getting to hounds was, I think, the most marvellous I have ever seen and the most successful.

"I remember once running up to Oundle Wood, at the side of which was a large moat, with an archway over, at the end of which were upright palings, bowed round on either side to prevent cattle from straying into the wood. From the top of the bridge to the water was a good depth. The colonel, when half-way over, found there was no way over the palings and he quietly and deliberately pulled his horse round, put his head for the water, and with a touch of the spur made him jump out into it. He plunged round the palings, up the bank into the wood and went on with the hounds, leaving every man standing in wonderment. Not one attempted to follow."

Another time, Tom and J.A.T. were together late in the afternoon "somewhere on the Wellingboro' side" when they came to a river. "Hounds had crossed and, as there did not appear to be a likely looking place handy by which we could follow them, the colonel

Figure 2.3 Dick Roake — first Whipper-in and Kennel Huntsman

21

said, 'Come on Tom. We shall both be drowned, but never mind.' We plunged in, but got safely over, although it was said afterwards — with a certain amount of exaggeration, of course — that it was forty feet deep where we crossed."

Tom's tribute to J.A.T. ended, "In addition to being a wonderful horseman, Colonel Thomson was the best huntsman I have ever seen. Everything was in order and done in a workmanlike manner, therefore there was no misunderstanding."

The feelings must have been mutual, for in his reminiscences J.A.T. disparages the horsemanship of his erstwhile huntsman, Charlie Payne, by comparison with Tom Firr. At the end of the 1868-69 season J.A.T. gave up the Mastership and Tom had to look for another berth. Tom's Pytchley admirers presented him with a silver hunting horn.

HUNTSMAN AT LAST

According to Tom, his departure for Kenilworth and the North Warwickshire, stepping up from second whipper-in to huntsman in one bound, happened by chance — just as a coincidence had led him to join the Pytchley. And the scales were tipped in his favour by Colonel Anstruther Thomson.

"Never having been a first whipper-in, I naturally had no thought of getting a huntsman's job," Tom wrote, modestly. "But when riding home after a day with the Oakley Hounds in Mr. Arkwright's time, I said by chance to the colonel, 'I hear they want a huntsman for the North Warwickshire, sir.' The immediate reply was, 'Have a cut for it, Tom. I'll back you.' Delighted with the idea, I accordingly applied for the post, and as Colonel Thomson sent a letter of recommendation at the same time, I had no difficulty in getting the job."

Mr. Richard Lant, of Nailcote Hall, Coventry, had taken the North Warwickshire in 1869, the year Tom joined them. The out-going Master, Mr. Oswald Milne, sold his pack — formed in 1862 — to his successor, and the huntsman, Robert Pattle, departed for the West Wilts. The Lant family knew J.A.T. very well, as he had hunted part of the North Warwick country during the first of his three Masterships of the Atherstone. Mr. Lant and many of his field were also acquainted with Tom Firr, having seen him in action around Crick and on the Pytchley "far Saturdays."

An echo of the Eglinton was to be found in the Kenilworth kennels, for the nucleus of the pack acquired by Mr. Lant came from the same Mr. Baker, the bloodhound man, whose influence could be seen in the Eglinton pack when Tom was in Scotland. Tom was fairly pleased with what he saw when he took up his first post as huntsman. But not all of Mr. Lant's hounds met with approval.

"A useful, hard-working lot they turned out to be, especially after weeding out one or two, which were much better at home than in the hunting field," Tom remarked. "One in particular, a dog called *Guider*, was mute as a maggot, in consequence of which terrible fault he frequently got away with the line of a fox by himself, thereby doing no end of harm. Yet strange to relate, he had got his name up as a first class foxhound. Everyone seemed to know *Guider*. But they shortly knew him no more!"

Among the more pleasant duties Tom had to perform as North Warwickshire huntsman was to attend a dinner given in honour of Colonel Anstruther Thomson at Northampton. The retired Master of the Pytchley was presented with a portrait of himself on his favourite hunter, *Iris*, painted by Sir Francis Grant. And Tom rounded off the evening by singing a song of his own composition, entitled *Iris*.

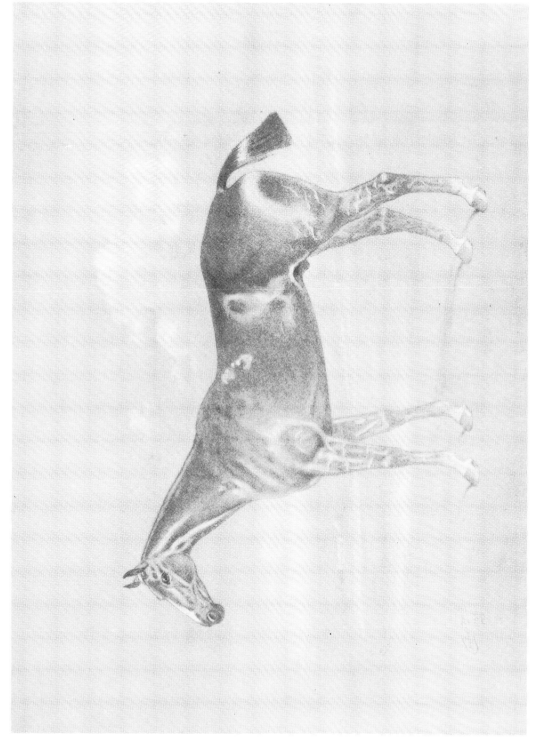

Figure 2.4   Fresco — Tom Firr's mount in the Waterloo Run

23

WARWICKSHIRE DAYS

In his description of the North Warwicks country, Tom said, "That part of it near Leamington was perhaps considered the most unfashionable, being considerably wooded. Yet it was very sporting, and good for hounds. Several coverts belonged to Lord Leigh (than whom there was no better fox-preserver), a find in any of them at any time being next to a certainty." Writing thirty years after he left Kenilworth, Tom went on, "The Birmingham side, for which I have always had a great liking, may by this time be much built upon with villa residences. Yet I have no doubt there is sufficient left for a good gallop to be seen in it, if not quite so thinly populated as it was in days gone by. I have seen some capital sport there, and I shall never forget going into it for the first time.

"The sportsmen from the hardware town are always keen, but they were perhaps more keen than usual on that occasion. It was October, and the first time hounds had been seen that season. We had a good morning's sport and, although the regular hunting had not begun, we were not confined to covert hunting but got away with a fox, eventually bowling him over in the open." Tom had good reason to remember that first outing on the Birmingham side. His reception by the field could not have been better and in his report of it he let slip, for once, his normal reticence, for Tom added, "The Birmingham gentlemen were so elated that, immediately after hounds had broken up their fox, one of them stood up in his stirrups and called, 'Three cheers for the new huntsman. He means business.' The cheers were most heartily given and, as may be imagined, I turned towards home with a cheerful countenance."

Another incident in the same line of country involved a mysterious horseman. "I remember one day on the Birmingham side noticing a strange gentleman out, wearing a most eccentric get-up: black trousers and black frock-coat, with a white neckcloth, and carrying an umbrella! He was mounted on a raw-boned, game-looking old steed. And there he sat in the pouring rain, beneath his umbrella, on the downwind side of Earl's Wood as hounds drew it. We were some time getting away. But the stranger in black was never off his guard, and when at last the start was made . . . he was one of the first away.

"The line hounds ran was a rough one but seemed wonderfully well suited to both horse and rider of whom I am writing, the frock-coat and black trousers disappearing through, or over, each succeeding scraggy fence in the most approved style. And so they continued, for there was a scent, and the style in which hounds ran and the country crossed in those forty-five minutes was never more suited to any man than to the stranger in black. I enquired several times, but never could make out who he was, or where he hailed from."

Tom continued, "Several very sporting runs have I seen on that side. One I remember, in which a rather pecular incident happened, was from Coleshill Pools. A rattling good fox was found there and, with a scent to suit them, hounds ran in rare style. A considerable part of the run was over the Atherstone country. We had been running for about fifty minutes and hounds had worked up pretty close to their fox, with *Duster*, a son of the Berkeley *Rioter*, running at their head with his hackles up, as he generally did with a sinking fox.

"A newly born lamb happened to be in the line and in *Duster*'s way, as he evidently thought, for I have never seen such a thing done before or since — he picked up the lamb, shook it once, chucked it over his shoulder and went about his business, with hackles

Figure 2.5 Detail of Temple's painting of the North Warwickshire, showing Tom Firr as Huntsman

25

erect as before! Mr. John Lant, who used to go well over a country, was with me at the time and, seeing Duster pick up something of a brown and yellow colour, thought it must be the fox and actually pulled up and holloa'd 'who-oop' before finding out his mistake. A short distance further on, and well into the Atherstone country, hounds ran into their fox and finished an excellent run.

"The result of this day's sport was a formal enquiry as to whom Coleshill Pools really belonged. For some reason it was said we had no right to draw the covert at all, the Atherstone Hunt laying claim to it as their own. Accordingly, the dispute was laid before the Masters of Foxhounds Committee at Boodle's, which, after carefully going into the matter, decided in favour of the North Warwickshire, so that Coleshill Pools continued to be drawn as before.

"Hay Wood, near Wroxhall Abbey, was a covert noted for its stout foxes, a kill being a rare occurrence. So much so that either Peter Collinson or George Boxall, I cannot remember which, had a knife handle made from the pad of a fox they killed from there. I remember killing a fox in the ruins of Kenilworth Castle, after a very good run from this covert; also others, equally good, each one a fine test of strength and cunning on the part of the fox.

"The Rugby, or Dunchurch, side of the North Warwickshire cannot be beaten, in my estimation. With its large tracts of grass and its small, well-kept coverts, it is very similar to the best part of its neighbours, the Pytchley, or Lord Willoughby de Broke's. All that is required is a good fox and, when that is forthcoming, then the success of the run is assured."

Good runs were *not* always assured and needed careful preparation. Tom explained: "As there were no foxes in Bunker's Hill the summer I went there, I asked for, and obtained, permission from Mr. Lant to dig out one of three litters in Kenilworth Chase Wood, which could easily be spared. Mr. Bullen, an excellent sportsman, who lived at Toft and farmed the land around the covert, was pleased to see me and the cubs — five beauties about three parts grown — and gave his shepherd strict instructions to take care of them and to act according to my directions.

"I put the cubs into the earth with a leash of rabbits and a tin of water, and drove stakes down at the mouth, giving the shepherd instructions to feed them every day on rats or rabbits and see that they had water. At the end of the week he was to pull up the stakes, come away from the covert and never go back to it again, and I have every reason to believe these instructions were strictly carried out.

"The cubs were marked and they did us rare service. The run from Bunker's Hill to Shuckborough on the first Thursday in November 1870 was with one of them, and that I look upon as one of the best gallops of twenty-seven minutes I have ever seen. The line was one of the finest that could be picked and must have been over more than eight miles of country at the least, and hounds had their fox dead on the lawn in front of the Hall in the time mentioned. As far as I can remember, Captain R. Soames, Captain Kennedy and Mr. John Arkwright, of Hatton, saw as much as anyone of this splendid gallop."

UNDERSTANDING THE FOX

From his childhood Tom followed the precept that to hunt a fox a man must understand its every move and should have the ability to think like a fox. He spent hours observing

Figure 2.6   John Chaworth Musters

how the animals behaved, noting their feeding habits, their ability to jump like a cat, sometimes clearing obstacles eight or nine feet high; the various ruses they employed to evade capture, including disguising their scent and running along the tops of walls; and the way a handsome brush, used as a rudder, helped a fox to twist and turn at seemingly impossible angles when going at full speed.

When he was a boy he watched a fox mouse-catching in a field on a summer evening, within twenty yards of the Puckeridge Kennels during Mr. Parry's Mastership. "Perfectly healthy, and sleek as a mole, there was pug, with wonderful agility springing from tuft to tuft, driving his nose into the sedgy grass, and at times picking up the tiny morsels which he seemed thoroughly to enjoy, notwithstanding that a note might occasionally be heard from one or more of the fifty couple who occupied the benches hard by."

An article written by Tom was evidence of his deep study of the subject and his respect, even affection, for foxes. He advised his readers how they might watch cubs at play in the spring or early summer. He gave an example of the consideration shown to a vixen with cubs. "I was once a good way forward, looking down a ride in a wood, the huntsman being almost out of my hearing, but not of an old vixen who came over the riding shortly after I arrived, with a cub in her mouth, stopping and turning her head to listen and then going on again. She evidently had her cubs above ground, and commenced to move them, as she thought, to a place of greater safety the moment she became aware of hounds in the neighbourhood. I at once informed the Master of the fact, and hounds were taken to another covert without delay."

In the same article he asserted that badgers were a great nuisance because they opened up earths that had been stopped and they killed cubs. "I know there are those who do not agree with me in this, but there are many who do. Old George Carter, of Tedworth fame, among others of great experience, always declared it, and I have myself on different occasions found dead cubs at the mouth of earths with tusk marks penetrating the brain, evidently from the chopping bite of the badger."

The hunting diaries which Tom Firr's family have treasured all these years begin with a brief note about his last season with the North Warwickshire. His first entry states: "Finished cubhunting Fri. Oct. 27th. 8 brace killed. 7 brace to ground. Commenced regular hunting Oct. 31st, Stoneleigh Abbey — a fair day and ran a brace to ground." Entries for individual days contain rather terse comments, such as, "No hounds could have hunted better." "Woodcote scarcely fit to ride." "A good day in the Pytchley country round back." Figures at the end show forty-one brace killed, twenty-eight to ground in sixty-three days' hunting in the 1871-72 season.

The diaries consist of seven notebooks with a total of 840 pages, covering about six thousand runs in three thousand days. While Tom's diaries start with the North Warwickshire, his memoirs end there. And he does not set out, in either the diaries or reminiscences, the background to the most important offer he received in his life — the Quorn as huntsman.

Peter Beckford's description of his paragon of a huntsman might well have been an inventory of Tom Firr's qualities.

"He should be young, strong, bold, and enterprising; fond of the diversion and indefatigable in the pursuit of it; he should be sensible and good-tempered; he ought also to be sober: he should be exact, civil and cleanly; he should be a good horseman and a good groom: his voice should be strong and clear; and he should have an eye so quick as to perceive which of his hounds carries the scent when all are running; and should have so excellent an ear as always to distinguish the foremost hounds when he does not see them: he should be quiet, patient and without conceit. Such as the excellencies which constitute a good huntsman: he should not be, however, too fond of displaying them until necessity calls them forth: he should let his hounds alone whilst they *can hunt*, and he should have genius to assist them *when they cannot*."

Add to all that a deep knowledge of the countryside and the ways of foxes, an iron nerve and the ability to out-ride any man over ground he knew like the back of his hand, and it is easy to see why Tom Firr was unmatched in his lifetime.

In his three years at Kenilworth Tom had shown good sport. His efficiency and horsemanship attracted the attention of the experts and he was picked out as the "coming huntsman" by Baily's Magazine, whose correspondent said of him, with remarkable insight, "Before many years he will be quite the head of his profession." John Coupland, who had taken the Quorn, went with his predecessor, the vastly experienced John Chaworth Musters, to cast an eye over Firr before an approach was made to him. The North Warwickshire parted with Tom regretfully, but on the best of terms. He was presented with a farewell gift of a fine silver cup.

★ ★ ★

Figure 2.7 Tom Firr as Huntsman

Figure 2.8   **Top:** Baggrave Hall   **Bottom:** Lowesby Hall

30

CHAPTER 3

CONQUISTADORS OF THE QUORN COUNTRY

BY GUY PAGET

(This description of the Quorn, which gives the background to Tom Firr's appointment, was written in 1951, shortly before Major Paget's death, and it is published for the first time by kind permission of his son, Lord Paget of Northampton).

Every jewel must have a setting to show it off to the best advantage. Tom Firr's achievements cannot be seen in their true perspective without some knowledge of the stage on which he acted, for the Quorn is quite unlike any other Hunt in England.

What is now called the Quorn is part of the country hunted in 1698 by Thomas Boothby, of Tooley Park, within Leicester Forest. When he died, after hunting his pack for fifty-five seasons, Hugo Meynell, a young Derbyshire squire of good fortune, took over Quorndon Nether Hall from Lord Ferrers and there, in 1753, established the first subscription pack of foxhounds. The country he hunted reached from Nottingham to Harborough, from Lutterworth to Melton, from Uppingham to Ashby-de-la-Zouch. It also took in part of Derbyshire.

During Meynell's time, the Enclosure Acts were sweeping away the open field system of agriculture. Fast riding and the flying leap were introduced as a consequence. To compete with these innovations, Meynell bred faster and faster hounds. Since his time, a Derby winner and a dozen Grand National winners have been pressed into the service of catching 'em. By 1800 there were three famous packs with which people hunted from Melton: the Duke's, or Belvoir; the Earl's, or Cottesmore; and the Squire's (in Meynell's and Osbaldeston's times), or Quorn. This last was sometimes called The Melton Hunt.

The history of the Quorn reads like that of Mexico. Ever since Meynell's time there had been a war between the foreign horsemen who rode victorious into Melton some time before 1800, and the "bally locals," sometimes called "Beasts of the Forest." These included the noble families of Hastings (of Ashby-de-la-Zouch); Grey (of Groby, Earls of Stamford), and Ferrers (of Staunton Harold), besides such local notables as the de Lisles of Garendon; the Herricks, of Beaumanor, and the Storys of Lockington.

At times the natives rebelled and established their own form of government west of the "Dixie line," running from Nottingham to Leicester. Occasionally one of them was elected Master of the Quorn but he was soon stabbed in the pocket, the general fate of those who aspired to that high position. Lord Stamford, the Master in 1856-63, realised he could not hold all he had conquered and allowed another native to set up an independent pack in the southern province known as the Harborough, or Billesdon, country. Both countries eventually fell to the conquistadors once more, but they have never been re-united.

The southern province remained under foreigners until the last few years, and very charming and efficient they were, but Lord Lonsdale was the last of the conquistadors at Quorn. Between 1800 and 1870 the Quorn had eighteen masters, fifteen of whom were foreigners, and there were almost as many new packs. The list of huntsmen, amateur and professional, contains some of the most famous names in fox-hunting — Mr. Assheton Smith, Squire Osbaldeston, Tom Sebright, Dick Burton, Sir Richard Sutton, John Treadwell, Mr. John Chaworth Musters and Frank Gillard.

FAME ON THE MELTON SIDE

The Quorn Hunt and Meltonia are two very different things. Firr had to deal with both. After it lost the Harborough side in 1857, the Quorn country was hunted four days a week, but only two of these were in areas that strangers think of as Leicestershire hunting country. The Charnwood Forest would be termed "rough" in any country outside Wales, and the Nottingham-Derby side is distinctly second-rate. What became known as the Monday and Friday side, however, is such a paradise that it pays for all — in more senses than one. On the Forest and to the north-west of Loughborough the field was only a handful of real hunting men. It was on the Melton side that Firr made his name famous the world over; but it was on the other side that he moulded the pack that was the basis of his renown. There he had plenty of room to watch and educate his hounds. There all their virtues and weaknesses were tested — nose, stoutness, soundness, and steadiness, for to kill their fox on the Forest hounds must hunt for themselves. Pace to race over the weak fences and rolling grass is the thing that matters on the Melton side, but there a huntsman cannot watch each hound as he is steeplechasing against a hundred foot-followers besides the riders.

I think it very doubtful if any pack of hounds round Melton, however numerous, could sustain the pressure of four days a week unless they had the Charnwood Forest, or the Cottesmore Woodlands, or the Lincolnshire fens to recuperate their twanging nerves. Hounds do not like being over-ridden and jumped on any more than we do, and unless they have days when they can hunt the fox without fear of their lives, it will not be long before they just run before the avenging horseman until either they or their pursuers are out of breath. Fortunately for the huntsman and for everyone else, including the conquistadors, no pack had to suffer the full Melton field more than two days a week at most. The Meltonian could hunt with the Quorn on Monday and Friday, with the Cottesmore on Tuesday, and with the Belvoir on Wednesday. On Thursday and Saturday, by going a little further, he could hunt with Mr. Tailby on the Harborough side.

It was on Saturday, a poor day with any of the Melton packs, that the non-subscribing native manufacturers, doctors, lawyers, local bankers, brewers and shopkeepers came out. Being locals, the second-rate was good enough for them! The hunting farmers had received more consideration when the Quorn days were mapped out. Melton market was on Tuesday, when the pack was far away on the Forest. Leicester corn market was on Saturday, when all hunting was beyond Loughborough. Leicester cattle market and Loughborough market on Wednesday and Thursday, both non-hunting days. Leicester Repository Sales, magistrates' courts and such things as County Council committee meetings were generally fitted in on non-hunting days, or on Saturdays and Tuesdays. Now, of course, it is all different, for most of the formerly glittering Meltonians are daily-

Figure 3.1 Melton Mowbray — the Pack in Cheapside

breaders and only week-end hunters. The true Meltonian six-days-a-week hunting man is dead as a Dodo.

For quite a big slice of Firr's time, the Quorn was more nearly the Melton Hunt than it had ever been, when the Donington country — the Saturday country and half the Charnwood Forest — was lent to Earl Ferrers, who hunted it separately. To make up for this, the Meltonians were given bye-days on Thursdays. The conquests of the Meltonians were made easier by the lack of big landowners. For a county of its size, there were amazingly few owners of, say, more than ten thousand acres in Leicestershire. Lord Stamford had been Master for a time and had had enough. The Marquis of Hastings had played the fool with the hunt for two seasons whilst he drank and gambled himself to death. The permanent resident peers could be counted on the fingers of one hand. In the seventies, the dominant personality was the 2nd Earl of Wilton, the King of Meltonia. The second son of Lord Grosvenor (Westminster), he was a Cheshire man on both sides. In Leicestershire, he owned only Egerton Lodge, a Melton villa, originally built about 1800 for Lord Darlington. But he and his fellow conquistadors ran the Quorn.

Meltonia was raised on the foundations of the ancient market town of the Mowbrays. It had been discovered, about 1790, by a Lambton of Durham, who came there for peace and quiet from the racket of Quorn and Loughborough. He was quickly followed by a band of pioneers composed of the bluest blood of many lands, with a good smattering of Napoleonic war profiteers and a few of Mr. Pitt's bounding baronets. When the sons and grandsons of these acquired the status of old county families, they looked down on the *nouveaux riches* of the industrial revolution.

Figure 3.2   Sir Richard Sutton

A FORMIDABLE CROWD

In 1870 Meltonia was still at its peak. Within its small compass there were between twenty and thirty hunting boxes, or lodges, bearing some of the oldest names in the peerage — Plymouth, Egerton, Cardigan, Craven, Warwick, Wicklow, Coventry, etc. — and more were going up each year. They were let for round about £1,000 a season. Many had stabling for twenty horses and more. The clubs which had been a feature of the old bachelor days were disappearing, but most of the houses within ten miles of Melton were let to hunting people. It was about this time that ladies of good position in society began to hunt, and to come to Melton, in any number. Up to Sir Richard Sutton's time at least, such ladies riding to hounds had been outnumbered by ladies of the other sort, such as Nellie Holmes and Skittles — so called because she once worked in a skittle alley — who caused a stir in the 1860s when she fell out with Lady Stamford.

The majority of the hunting tenants were young, rich and keen, but many were ignorant as far as hunting was concerned. They wanted twenty-five minutes of the best in the morning, and again in the afternoon. Sir Richard Sutton once asked a "Spring Captain" to avoid jumping on *Searcher* and *Virtue*. "Sorry," was the reply, "but I've such a damn bad eye for a hound, I'm afraid they must take their chance with the rest!"

On Fridays there would be three hundred horsemen out. To be fair, although they were less aristocratic, they were not as bad as those of Squire Osbaldeston's period. Sir Richard Sutton and Lord Stamford had dealt faithfully with them and Mr. Clowes was not slow in turning gamekeeper. Even the worst offenders recognised that Lord Hastings' mob-rule was hopeless and almost welcomed the firm hand of Chaworth Musters and his pupil, John Coupland.

Moreton Frewen, of Cold Overton, gave a reasonable picture of the mid-Victorian Meltonians, contrasting the majority with one of the few real fox-hunters. He said, "it used to delight Tom Firr to see The Squire (Henry Chaplin) about, for he was as knowledgeable on the flags as in the field. Of us, not one in a hundred knew Quorn Alfred when we saw him; but this visitor had patted the great hound at kennel shows innumerable. And because Firr was pleased, his hounds seemed to know it and were thus a little quicker than ever to get out of covert. Looking back on it all, Firr must have thought very little of us young fellows. For hounds we cared not a jot; they existed just to give us a direction towards which we pointed our horses' heads."

They were a formidable crowd to have to compete with. The Pytchley White Collar Boys were a bit wild, but there were not so many of them. They were, *en masse*, friends not rivals. They were not so well mounted, nor so ignorant. The Quorn country favoured the horses far more than the Pytchley did. The Birmingham Boys of the Warwickshire were rough, but they were not mounted on Derby and National winners and were few in number compared to the Meltonians of the '70s. However little the Meltonians knew about hunting hounds, they were expert and severe critics of riding to them. There was Mr. Wilson on Father O'Flynn; and there was Harry Custance, the champion flat-race jockey, on that marvellous hunter, The Doctor, which had run second in the Grand National. Lord Wilton and his son had thirty or forty of their three-hundred guinea hunters at Egerton Lodge. The Behrens brothers had even more costlier ones, with Captain "Doggie" Smith, the best amateur rider, to keep them tuned to concert pitch.

The doings of the Quorn field were news, and the news was published to the world by

Figure 3.3 The Squire — Henry Chaplin

the best of them. Captain Pennell-Elmhirst hunted from Brooksby Hall, which was rented by his brother-in-law, Mr. Ernest Chaplin (of whom it was said that he came there with twelve horses and no children and left with twelve children and no horses). Each week in The Field, over the name of Brooksby, Elmhirst recorded the doings of the Melton packs in inimitable prose. Brooksby himself was a first-class man to hounds and had hunted the Woodland Pytchley. He never mentions a hound by name, and seldom the huntsman, but in the last chapter you will find yourself sailing after him, hot and breathless, through rasper, rails and brooks. But no picture of the chief actor, Tom Firr; only of where and how his followers went.

Figure 4.1   Mr J. Coupland — Master of the Quorn in 1872

CHAPTER 4

MR. COUPLAND TAKES A HAND

When Tom Firr arrived at Quorndon with his wife and young family in 1872 he was thirty-one years old, with the experience of nine situations spread over fifteen years in a variety of countries and under widely different Masters. His frame had not an ounce of spare flesh. He weighed around nine stones and stood about five feet eight inches; wiry and strong and with a quick eye, a musical voice, a good brain and an iron nerve. His face was generally solemn — indeed he had been likened to an archbishop — but his twinkling eyes betrayed a keen sense of humour. Like all great sportsmen, he was fastidious about his dress and equipment: his stock always looked as if it had been carved from marble, his coat was spotless and his boots shone like mirrors.

Lady Augusta Fane, who saw him hunt hounds for many years, described him thus: "In appearance, Firr closely resembled a fox. He had a sharp, thin face and clear, keen eyes, and nothing escaped his notice. His hounds loved and trusted him implicitly, obeyed the slightest wave of his hand and flew back to work at the sound of his inspiring voice that set the blood coursing through one's veins and made the most timid rider ready and anxious to jump the biggest fence."

But even the best of huntsmen can have his work marred by an unsympathetic Master. Teamwork is essential for good sport. In Firr's case, he was fortunate in having Mr. Coupland, following in the shadow of Mr. Chaworth Musters.

IN FRANK GILLARD'S FOOTSTEPS

Mr. Coupland, a ship-owner whose home was in Cheshire but who hunted regularly from Melton, had nearly acquired the Quorn pack in 1866, at the end of Mr. Clowes's Mastership. The pack was on offer to Mr. Coupland for £1,500, which he was prepared to pay if he could get a guaranteed subscription. No such guarantee was given, so he waited for four years, and two Masterships, before taking over.

The first of those intervening Masters was the Marquis of Hastings, who bought twenty-eight couple of the hounds and set about hunting the north Quorn country. Harry Hastings had succeeded to the title when he was nine years old. He led a profligate, madcap life and was well on the way to ruin when he died, aged twenty-six. The Quorn also went downhill for two years because of his capricious behaviour, inspiring a mocking verse which summed up the Hunt's plight. It began:

> When will the Marquis come? Who can tell?
> Half past twelve or half past one — who can tell?
> Is he sober, is he drunk, nipping like Mynheer Van Dunk?
> Will he ride, or will he funk? Who can tell?

Two years of mismanagement cannot ruin the traditions built up by a Hunt like the Quorn, nor spoil its country. The speedy manner in which its good name was restored owed much to the Master who followed, of whom Colin Ellis wrote: "Although Mr. Chaworth Musters only hunted for two season, I think he must be ranked as one of the great figures in the history of the Quorn Hunt. He not only provided sport, he promoted good feeling and he paved the way for the setting up of a new system."

Mr. Musters had been Master of the South Notts and he took his own pack with him to the Quorn, hunting the Donington side himself and leaving the fashionable Melton side to that outstanding huntsman Frank Gillard.

When ill health forced him to retire temporarily (he surfaced again as the South Notts Master from 1871 to 1876), Mr. Musters made sure he had a successor ready to take over — Mr. Coupland. The outgoing Master also lent his hounds to Mr. Coupland for the 1870-71 season, to enable him to get to know the country better and to organise a subscription pack.

Although he was not a Leicestershire man, the Quorn took to Mr. Coupland. Forty-six years old, he had hunted fairly regularly with the Cheshire packs and, as already indicated, was not unknown at Melton. His knowledge of hounds stemmed from a pack he kept in India as a young man, hunting jackal or anything else they could find on the outskirts of Bombay. On his return to England he was schooled in the finer points of fox-hunting by Walker, Sir Watkin Williams-Wynn's huntsman. Also in Mr. Coupland's favour was his apparent prosperity, for his Liverpool shipping business was thriving and he kept twenty-five horses in the Quorn country.

Frank Gillard stayed on as huntsman for Mr. Coupland's first season, at the end of which Gillard went on to distinguished service with the Belvoir. His successor, James MacBride, was the son-in-law of Tom Day, the former Quorn huntsman. And it was from MacBride that Tom Firr took over. Tom wrote of him, "It is often said that however good a man may be as a whipper-in, he does not always make a good huntsman, and probably the same may be said of James MacBride, for I think I am right in saying he never did shine as a huntsman, although a better man to turn a hound never need be wished for.

"No fence was too big for him. If duty called him to the other side his whole mind was in his work and, being quick as lightning, he was always likely to give satisfaction to any man who had the command of his assistance."

Tom Firr was not alone in thinking that MacBride lacked the essential qualities. In the words of The Field, he was "found lacking in the peculiar talent of grappling with the overgrown crowds of the Shires."

Firr discovered that little had changed in the nine years since his sojourn as the Quorn's second whipper-in. Melton was still the centre of things. It was a pleasant market town, with bow windowed shops. Many of the front doors were split, like stable doors, so that the upper parts could be opened on fine days while the lower portions remained shut, to

Figure 4.2　Mary Hannah Firr — Wife of Tom

41

keep out stray dogs and the parade of animals to and from the market.

The town was the Mecca of fox-hunters. It had endured a reputation for attracting hard-riding young rakes in the early years, but gradually an air of maturity spread and ladies were to be seen out riding with their husbands.

Tom also found that the country itself had altered hardly at all. Most of the enclosing had been done in the first half of the century, land had been drained and wire introduced.

The fences evolved over a number of years, providing obstacles of varying stiffness. The thorn, when first planted, was protected by post and rails on either side, with a ditch. This was a formidable obstacle when the rails were new and sturdy. In about eight years the thorn fence was cut and laid and a hedge grew up that would turn over any horseman who tried to go through it. After another ten years the old layers would be dying and young shoots from the base developed into a tall bullfinch, through which the fox-hunter could force a way. At this stage the vigour of the fence would be revived by cutting and laying again. So the cattle were kept in, and the fox-hunter's mettle was tested by an interesting succession of fences. But there were people hunting with Tom Firr who could remember when there was not a single fence between Nottingham Castle and Belvoir Castle.

★   ★   ★

A ROYAL ENCOUNTER

Some of Tom's friends had advised him that he should not give up his position with the North Warwickshire, in which he was a proven success, for the most difficult of huntsmen's posts. But he knew in his heart he was tailor-made for the Quorn. He must have had some trepidations about becoming the third huntsman of Mr. Coupland's first three years as Master. Tom's hunting diaries add no colour to the start of their partnership, which lasted for twelve years. There is a diary note that the Quorn began cub-hunting on 29 August 1872, at Quorn Wood. On the last day of the year there was "not much sport," and they "drew a lot of Lord Stamford's coverts blank." On 3 January 1873, from Gt. Dalby, they "stopped hounds after 3h. 45m." A week later, Tom stated cryptically: "Field behaved badly so we stopped hounds." He recorded forty-one brace killed and eighteen to ground in 139 days that season.

Soon after taking up his new duties, Tom had a reminder that the Quorn huntsman needed to be at ease with people from all social levels. The Prince of Wales visited Melton Races and attended a meet at Gaddesby. When Tom was presented, the prince remarked that they had first met at Savernake during a day with the Tedworth, to which Tom replied, "Beg pardon, Your Royal Highness, before that — when I was with the Cambridgeshire."

"Oh yes," said Prince Edward, "you were the boy on old John Press's second horse. They jumped better for you than they did for him. What fun we had!"

Tom and his wife settled down quickly at Quorn, where they had a pleasant home close to the church at which they worshipped each Sunday. Mary Firr was a tremendous help to Tom in that transitional period. She came from an old Northamptonshire family. On her mother's side she was descended from the Langton-Freemans, squires of Wilton, near Daventry, as far back as 1644. Her paternal line, the Knights, is not so clear, but one would like to think she numbered among her ancestors the 18th century Pytchley huntsman, Dick Knight.

By the end of that first season Tom's position was secure and he had already begun to put the stamp of his personality on the Quorn. Brooksby confirmed Tom Firr's mastery in one paragraph in December 1873: "Go and place yourself where you have seen a fox stealing across the main ride of Walton Thorns, and get two yards to leeward of Tom Firr as he cheers them to the cry. If it doesn't make a boy of you, it will make you an old woman on the spot. You must either stiffen in your saddle with concentrated excitement, or you must turn round and cry over your dotage. Huic! huic! huic! Yo-oi! a'at him there, old bitches! Yo-'o'i!! (Santley hasn't a note approaching it)."

Each year the hunt staff received new horses, for Mr. Coupland's business instincts resulted in an annual sale. The sale in May 1873 brought in 5,836 guineas for forty-six hunters, an average of almost 127 guineas. Meltonians at one time grumbled that the Master was running the Hunt at a profit when they were asked to increase their subscriptions. But it is clear Mr. Coupland had a good eye for a horse. He bought *Pathfinder* for his huntsman and it later won the Grand National for Lord Huntly, who had given £1,200 for it. *Pathfinder*, of course, was not the only National winner to go out with the Quorn. He was, however, particularly well named. His jockey, Pickernell, drank so heavily before the race that he arrived at the start at a loss to know which way to go along the Aintree course. Pickernell quickly sobered up during the race and won cleverly from Dainty by half a length.

*   *   *

QUORN ALFRED ARRIVES

Fortunately, the pack had been hunted by Tom's predecessor for only one season and had not become too set in their ways or too attached to one man. A year of being galloped over by the Quorn "cavalry" of two or three hundred was said, ironically, to have taught the hounds to keep clear and to have done wonders for their pace. The nucleus of Mr. Coupland's pack was the one he bought from the Craven, supplemented by a draft from the Belvoir.

In the year that Firr arrived, Mr. Coupland bought a whelp called *Alfred*, destined to become Tom Firr's pride and joy and the winner of the Stallion Hound Class and Champion Cup at York Hound Show in 1875. *Alfred* also won his class at the Alexandra Palace Show that year. His distant pedigree included Lord Henry Bentinck's *Contest*, Brocklesby *Rallywood* and Osbaldston's *Furrier*, but he had been bred from a Craven bitch named *Affable* and his sire was Mr. Garth's *Painter*. To Tom Firr he was the ideal twenty-four inch doghound; white-faced and roan colouring. The use of *Alfred* and Lord Coventry's *Rambler* were cited as instances of Bentinck influence in the Quorn pack during Firr's time. The arrival of *Alfred* as a whelp, not long after the new huntsman reached Quorndon, had an almost mystical touch about it and gave to the Quorn the last of the ingredients needed to guarantee a truly great decade.

Mr. Coupland, in casting about for hounds, took John Walker with him to Mr. Garth's kennel. There they were "much enraptured" by a beautiful young hound called *Painter*. As Guy Paget explained, "The next day, when inspecting the Craven pack,

43

Figure 4.3   Quorn Alfred — from a pencil drawing by Tom Firr

Affable was also admired," and being available at the time was sent to *Painter*. She did not come to Quorndon, but had her whelps in Berkshire, and *Alfred* was sent to his new home in a basket.

"Quorn *Alfred* did not escape the attention of the late Lord Willoughby de Broke, as the four litters by *Alfred* in 1878 and 1879 were virtually the foundation of the Warwickshire pack. Mr. Oakeley, of the Atherstone, used him extensively, as also did Sir Bache Cunard and Charles Leedham, of the Meynell. He was almost the corner-stone of his own kennel. As he was such a good all-round hound in the opinion of Tom Firr, and such a typical Leicestershire hound, he was bred from in his second season. By the time he was five years old there were eight couples by him on the Quorndon benches."

Alfred's sons included *Agent*, *Coroner*, *Woldsman*, and *Whynot*, stallion hounds of note; and among his daughters were *Alice*, *Adelaide*, *Dewdrop*, *Comely*, *Gay Lass*, *Gadfly* and *Waspish*, all dams of good hounds.

Lord Coventry's *Rambler* provided another strong branch for the pack to build on. And the Belvoir *Watchman*, by *Rallywood* the son of *Senator*, was very much used for three or four seasons. Over the years, Mr. Coupland brought in the Oakley *Danger*, Mr. Tailby's *Struggler* (said to be one of the best hounds seen in Leicestershire), Sir Watkin Williams-Wynn's *Challenger*, the Fitzwilliam *Brusher* and the Grafton *Silence*. They made a magnificent pack, fit for the king of huntsmen. And *Alfred* was not the only Quorn winner. *Rattler*, *Watchman*, *Comrade*, followed by *Governor*, *Woodman*, *Wildboy*, *Alice* and *Rapid*, collected prizes all over the country.

The introduction of showing (Peterborough Show did not start until 1878) was not entirely to Tom Firr's taste. He believed an emphasis on prize-winning characteristics could be detrimental to a breed, and might not help them in the jobs for which they were bred. Mr. Coupland, however, encouraged the trend and in his first year, 1870, he instituted the Quorn Puppy Show.

The annual shows later became useful to Firr because they brought him in close touch with the farmers. But a guide to his real feelings was given by a sketch he made in coloured crayons, of two Quorn hounds, under which he recorded their imaginary conversation:

> "Well, Rattler, my boy, safe back from the show?"
> "Yes, easily won the first prize, you know,
> For the moment I came to the front
> There was not another in the hunt!"
> "Pooh! pooh! my dear boy, now don't be vain
> It is deeds, not looks, that make a name,
> And if your deeds should prove evil,
> With all your good looks — you'll go to the devil!"

★ ★ ★

GALLOPING CASTS

Most of the followers who revelled in the fast runs provided by Tom Firr did not stop to question how they came about. Some of the jealous ones muttered that half the Quorn gallops were not after the fox, but were after Tom Firr. The sneer arose from Tom's galloping casts forward, a tactic he justified repeatedly, not in words but in results.

When hounds had made their own cast, Firr would move in the direction in which he intended to make his cast, perhaps giving a faint call, or a whistle, just enough to attract attention without putting hounds off. Then, according to scent, he would increase his pace, letting nothing obstruct him. Sometimes the foot followers would get in the way, threatening to head the fox and foil the line and to get hounds' heads up by their noise. Then Tom would make his casts wider; and wider still when, in the nineties, people were out in their hundreds on bicycles. He was accused of going away with too few hounds. And when asked with how many hounds would he choose to go away, he was said to have answered: "I don't know, sir, I just blow my horn when the fox goes away, and in two fields they are generally all there."

Once, after a fine run, Tom was able to demolish his critics without saying a word. A bob-tailed fox was found in Holwell Mouth, a crafty customer well known to the Quorn and the Belvoir. Hounds ran at a spanking pace to Little Belvoir, and then slightly slower uphill towards Cant's Thorns. There bob-tail lay in the covert, but not for long. Kettleby village was the next target. The huntsman took hounds clear of the village and then began a hard run past Old Hills and Scalford Spinney and on to plough, which enabled some of the straggling field to catch up. Firr held them forward on to grass and away they went for Freeby Wood, where an over-anxious sportsman headed the fox into covert. Only Firr's skill enabled them to hold on to the fox and back they went across the valley, past Chadwell, when a halloa brought them up again.

The next two miles were covered at racing pace, to the right of Clawson Thorns, running from scent to view and bowling over a game fox which had gone for two hours and fifteen minutes. Up came the know-alls, making the hackneyed charge that Tom had

Figure 4.4   Tom Firr with John Coupland at a Brooksby Meet (1873-74 season)

changed foxes. Furthermore they claimed he had "stumbled on the poor beggar" when the fox was asleep. The huntsman said nothing. He simply turned and held up bob-tail's three-inch stump of brush.

The rapport between Firr and his hounds acted like an invisible cord and resulted from devoted care. He had no need to shout; they seemed to know his every thought. Miss Evelyn Firr, his daughter, said the only thing that counted to him was his hounds. "Father would sit for hours, just looking at them without a word. For years he never took a holiday and hated to be even one night without his darlings." She added, on another occasion, "He had a tremendously strong will — I think this accounted, partly, for the great control which he had over animals."

An example of Tom's determination and control was given by Claude Luttrell, of Dunster, talking about his first fast hunt with the Quorn. Mr. Luttrell was impressed at the way hounds "came right through the field to join the leading hounds and then went screaming along without the semblance of a check." And also "the way Tom Firr, who hadn't got out of covert till we were well under way, seemed to swoop down on the leaders and was in front with his hounds all the way."

Tom Firr and Frank Freeman both cast hounds in front of them like a fan and never needed them to be driven with rating and whip-cracking. The spectacular galloping casts accomplished by Tom were possible only because of his wonderful intuition and the pack's complete faith in him. Lack of success would soon have ruined the pack. He was always full of sympathy for the hounds and spoke to them rather as one might address an intelligent young person. If he had to give up his fox, he dismounted and talked to the hounds in a soft, reassuring voice, with many a "bad luck, old fellow" and "no fault of yours." They seemed to understand and waved their sterns.

A further demonstration of the bond came at the closing stages of a very fast gallop, which ended in the neighbourhood of Welby after dark. The pack had raced ahead in the murky evening. Distant sounds, and then silence, told the tale and Tom blew his horn to call hounds back. After a few minutes, *Ruby*, a bitch descended from Quorn *Alfred*, came through a fence and placed the fox's mask at the huntsman's feet, and looked up at him, as if to say that they could do the job by themselves when necessary.

In a comment on Tom's method, Guy Paget wrote: "Much as Firr liked blood, he was scrupulously fair. No mobbing, or nicking and, above all, no bagmen! A hundred years ago bagged foxes were almost reckoned warrantable warren, or fair game, but as men became more civilised and hunting more a game than a profession, so were the rules stretched on the side of the fox, until today, when he's a good ten to one favourite every time. Bagmen lead to nicking and doping (slitting a pad or putting a smelling mixture on the fox) when liberated or bolted from an artificial earth. If it is done often enough, hounds will not hunt a clean one."

Digging was also anathema to Tom. "His hounds were never short of blood, so it was only necessary when a notorious outlaw slipped into the nearest drain," said Major Paget. "The village outlier is no good to man or hound and deserves no law. He generally spreads mange, runs up the poultry bill, causes the murder of honest foxes and never gives a hunt. But let this be said — in nine cases out of ten he is the victim of foul play, snares, traps or gunshots. That is what turns a fox into a criminal."

Tom Firr's remarkable voice has already been mentioned. He was also unusual in the variation of notes he sounded on his horn. Lady Augusta Fane described some of them

47

thus: "There was one very gay note when hounds were breaking out of covert; a sad one when the fox was lost, a steadying note when drawing a wood, and a most dismal note, only heard on the last day of the season, when he and his hounds returned to the kennels and it was 'good-bye' till the following September."

No one would claim that Tom was the most prolific fox-killer of all time. His average was about one a day. An assessment of seven years, taken at random, showed 548 killed in 605 days. But the mere statistics give no indication of the sport enjoyed and the total would have been much higher if Tom had not been so honest in his method.

There were, of course, less publicised factors which played a part in the almost guaranteed good sport to be seen with the Quorn. Mr. Coupland worked tirelessly behind the scenes to improve the country, focussing much of his attention on the improvement of the coverts, under the expert guidance of his huntsman. Earth-stopping had been expensive and inefficient, so Mr. Coupland called a meeting at which he offered ten shillings a find. But no pay was to be given to a keeper if a fox went to ground in a registered earth within his march. Earth-stoppers' dinners were held at Willoughby, Gaddesby and Loughborough, and Mr. Coupland handed out £250 for five hundred finds. After each of the dinners Tom Firr sang songs of his own composition. He also used the occasions to hear grievances from farmers, a public relations exercise that reaped dividends.

A DUCKING AT HOBY MILL

A bad fall over a brook kept Tom out of the saddle for a short time in the 1873-74 season. He had recovered when hounds ran to Hoby Mill, where Captain Arthur "Doggie" Smith led his horse over a shaky plank bridge, watched by his rival, a Radical M.P. called Tomkinson, from Cheshire. Once the rivals were safely over, Lord Grey de Wilton started across the rickety bridge, followed by George Moore, of Appleby. Then up galloped the Belvoir chaplain, a most jealous rider. He crashed into Moore, who cannoned on to Lord Grey de Wilton in the middle — and down went the bridge. His lordship, at the bottom of the pile, was knocked under by each horse in turn, but riders and horses all got out unhurt.

Tomkinson was also the leading actor in a tale which has appeared in many versions and with many alleged participants. We shall stick to Brooksby's version, as related to Ikey Bell, which has "Timber" Powell and Mr. Tomkinson ("Jumpkinson of the Cheshire") as the jealous protagonists.

One day Firr came to an impenetrable bullfinch. Tomkinson was close to him. Firr pulled up and said, "What bad luck Captain Powell is not out, he would have bored a hole through this." "Oh, would he?" said Tomkinson. Hard at it he went and fell, making a gap. Firr thanked him, and rode on.

Isaac Bell, as few will need reminding, was a Master and huntsman who was in the front rank of foxhound breeders. But when he first met Tom Firr, towards the end of Tom's life, Ikey was, in his own words, "an overgrown and delicate lad" whose single thought was to hunt hounds. He asked Firr, "Is it desperate hard on one hunting hounds four days a week; do you ever feel bad from it?" "Oh no," replied the huntsman. "Only thing I ever get is a bad cold, and I feel it riding to the meet, but the moment hounds find, and I have given a halloa or two and a blast on the horn, it's wonderful how it all clears up!"

Figure 4.5 The Ducking — Lord Grey de Wilton and others (1873–74 season)

During previous Masterships the failure of the Quorn committee to take decisive action had threatened the very existence of the Hunt. Mr. Coupland received a guarantee of £2,500 and a promise of £250 for a covert fund. He supplemented that with a steady flow of cash from his own pocket, and the fund was nearly £1,000 in debt to him by February 1874. Most of the coverts had been kept in good order, however.

The season of 1874-75 got off to a dreadful start, with Mr. Coupland hurting himself in a bad fall on 7 November, Tom Firr breaking his collarbone on 11 November and then, thirteen days later, Mrs. Coupland died. There was no hunting for a fortnight while the Master was in mourning. Setbacks continued into the New Year. On 5 February Tom noted, "Very good run was spoilt by Dick Webster continually nicking in and over-riding hounds." Three days later, "Mr. C. was huntsman on account of my unfortunate back being bad." Tom returned to duty on 11 February, but the frost lingered and he wrote in his diary, "Ground a great deal too hard. Lamed a great many hounds." All in all, it was a season to forget.

Such a spate of ill luck could not last, and the following year was remarkable for a number of splendid runs, which had Tom enthusing, "A very capital season." At the end of it, Colonel (later General) E. S. Burnaby, of Baggrave, presented a silver teapot, inscribed: "To Mr. T. Firr, in remembrance of some brilliant runs of The Quorn Season 1875-6." The dates of the runs formed a girdle round the pot.

The Duke of Portland was among those who heaped praise on the huntsman, "the best I have ever seen, and I believe no better rider to hounds ever lived." According to the duke, "His hands were like silk, his seat as firm as iron, and his voice was the most beautiful and electrifying that I have ever heard. His cheer to the hounds brought them rushing to him and inspired the field to deeds of extra valour."

The duke referred to Tom's dry humour. "My brother, Bill Bentinck, was with Tom near Little Belvoir when they came upon some hedgecutters making the fences very high and strong. With a sardonic grin Tom remarked, 'Why don't you make them a bit higher and stronger?' and disappeared over the top.

"However fast the hounds might run Tom Firr was hardly ever out of the same field with them, and he never seemed in a hurry. He sailed over the fences as if they were nothing. I well remember his jumping in succession three extremely ugly-looking hog-backed stiles. He passed over them as though they were sheep hurdles. The last one had a wide ditch and a footboard on the take-off side, with an ox-rail on the far side, and I did not see anyone else attempt it. But he made simply nothing of it.

"I followed him one day through a farmyard, and we turned into a grass field together. Tom jumped a big stake and bound fence, and I went after him. When in the air, I saw with horror a big, new ox-rail. My horse, *Doncaster*, smashed the ox-rail to smithereens, with a loud crack, but fortunately did not fall. The hounds checked in the field, and Tom, with a broad grin on his face, said, 'Is that you, Your Grace? I thought the noise was a cannon going off!'"

Tom told Lord Willoughby de Broke of an incident which occurred when hounds were running hard and reached a swollen brook. A horse in front of Tom stopped short and the rider was thrown head first into the icy stream. As Tom sailed overhead, the man lifted his face above the water and raised a smile by calling, "Cuckoo, cuckoo!"

On another occasion Tom himself was drenched. Borderer, in Baily's Magazine, confirming the huntsman's good humour, saw the look of disgust on Tom's face as he was thrown into Twyford Brook, only to surface with a smile, saying, "I could hear you laughing, captain, while I was still under the water."

Usually, when he fell Tom, like most fine riders in the hunting field, tended to receive a severe injury. Only about a dozen falls were recorded in twenty-eight years, in almost all of which he was hurt. He suffered concussion, he broke collar bones two or three times, he dislocated a knee and, in the most widely discussed of his falls, he fractured his skull. He also for years bore with fortitude a very painful back complaint, which on some days must have made riding an absolute agony.

An increasing use of wire in the second half of the century added to the hazards, especially when it was used in hedges to make a stronger barrier. Tom had a bad fall in February 1876 through getting tangled up with his horse in a wire fence which had been stretched down a drive near Thurnby. At first, the wire used in Leicestershire was not of the barbed variety but was plain, about a quarter of an inch thick. Fences made from it could be seen perfectly well if they stood on their own. The main danger came when the wire was hidden inside a hedge, or placed on the blind side.

The County Gentleman reported a January incident:

"We moved on to Thrussington Wolds ... then away over the road, pointing for Thrussington, and not far from this place Tom Firr got the most infernal fall that ever was seen. He was galloping fast in a grass field, and downhill, when his horse either put his foot in a hole, or blundered over a moleheap, which are numerous in many fields about here. He came down on his head, and after sliding for some distance, rolled completely over on his rider, who had not left the saddle, and apparently burying him into the earth. Another roll and the horse was off him, when we were all pleased to see him get up, not much damaged except the wind slightly knocked out..."

The reference to Tom not leaving the saddle is interesting because, of course, that reflex of an exceptional rider has been the cause of so many serious accidents. A not-so-good rider, with a light seat and firm hands, would have been thrown clear and probably turned on to his shoulders by his grip on the reins.

Against the Kirby Gate meet on 4 November 1878, Tom wrote in his diary, "Most unfortunate for me. Got into a brook on the Friday, which brought on rheumatism in my weak back and prevented me hunting the first week."

A month later, another diary entry states: "Hard frost. Not fit to hunt. Sad news to make matters worse, death of Major Whyte-Melville, having broken his neck." It was the sporting author Whyte-Melville, years before, who had drawn Brooksby's attention to the Pytchley whipper-in by shouting at a crowd in a gateway, "Room for Tom Firr! We can't do without him."

Mr. Coupland married again, after the death of his first wife, and in October 1879 Tom noted, "John o'Gaunt. Bagged a badger. Unfortunate accident to Mrs. Coupland, who jumped out of the carriage Mr. Coupland was driving, through one of the horses turning awkward, and broke her leg."

A full recital of the runs recorded by Tom in his diaries is impracticable, but a sample gives the flavour: "Saturday 17th Jan. 1880. Dishley Toll Gate. Found in Oakley Wood, ran by Hathern. From Hathern and Dishley back through Oakley and Piper woods away for Hookhill and then by Grace Dieu over Sharpley Rocks, by the monastery and reformatory, by Green Hill, then through Birch Hill and Copt Oak Wood and straight away for Markfield, by Shaw Lane, to Bawdon Hill. Then to the right to Copt Oak

Figure 4.6 Cuckoo, Cuckoo (see Text)

Church, through Poultney Wood, by Ulverscroft Abbey, to Black Hill.

"Then to Bawdon Castle and the Beacon to Whittle Mill, through the privets and away across Garendon Park. Then to Shepshed village, where the fox came away in view and ran through the Hermitage and on to Oakley Wood. Straight through this to Piper Wood and as far as Belton, and got to ground in a drain twenty yards in front of hounds, from which he was soon got out and eaten. Time four hours and a quarter. Distance 26 miles. Fine hunting run. Horses all beat. Lord Ferrers, Mr. W. Paget and myself saw the finish."

Tom's diaries, obviously, were not meant for the general reader. They were the inventories of his business, which was fox-hunting. Moreover, the entries were completed at a close of a hard day's work. When he came to write in the Loughborough Herald, the Leicester Chronicle, the County Gentleman, or other journals, his style was much more free and easy and more often than not he lapsed into verse.

In September, 1880, Tom allowed himself a diary comment on the weather conditions at Baggrave. "The wildest and roughest day ever witnessed. Trees blown in all directions, in fact torn up by their roots, scarcely allowing us to sit in our saddles. Of course, very little good could be done hunting."

A little later, a meet at Beeby attracted the comment:

> "Riders were fretting, their nags in a lather,
> Blowing and stopping to left and to right.
> Tails quickly shaking, each fence they were breaking,
> While the keen, spotted beauties ran clean out of sight."

52

Figure 4.7 Lord Willoughby de Broke

53

Now and again the railway lines caused havoc, and several hounds were killed by trains. Foxes seemed to have a canny understanding of the value of the railways in hampering a chase. One January, Tom "stopped hounds after a good run, by the railway at Plumtree, as the fox kept continually crossing and recrossing the railway and hounds were more than once nearly cut to pieces by the trains." But another, less agile customer was knocked silly by a train. That hunted fox was picked up off the line and placed in a bag for the journey to the kennels, where he was nursed back to health and then turned down at Baggrave.

"There is nothing so dreadful that I can think of as to see a train go thundering through a pack of hounds," reflected Tom, on a day in which one of his best hounds was killed. "Some engine drivers are very careful fellows. They are quick at seeing hounds on the line or approaching it; they are quick, too, at shutting off steam and applying the brake. They deserve to be, and are in most cases, rewarded. But the man who runs through: oh, horror! It was on Friday that this happened, in a run from Gartree Hill. Hounds were seen to be knocked up like ninepins when crossing the line, but luckily only one was killed."

Even Tom found advantages in the railway. At the conclusion of a particularly strenuous day, which saw him far from home with tired horses, he said: "I finished on Captain Elmhirst's, which he kindly lent me. Came home by train from Melton."

★ ★ ★

Figure 5.1 The problem of the railway (between Whissendine and Ashwell, 1878-79)

CHAPTER 5

TROUBLE AHEAD

The spreading octopus of the railways had an irreversible effect on both the country itself and on the composition of the field. Although the first line, between Leicester and Swannington, was opened in 1832, before Tom was born, the real impact of the improvement in communications was felt during his years with the Quorn. In 1840 the Midland Line from Derby to Leicester was opened, and through an extension to Rugby connected Loughborough and Leicester to London. Another eight years elapsed before the link from Syston to Peterborough was built, opening the way to Melton and Oakham. The connections with the Quorn country were improved in 1857 and 1868. And then, in 1879, a completely new line from Market Harborough to Melton was established, providing a through service to Euston. That was followed in 1880 by the opening of the much faster service to St. Pancras.

An obvious change was the quite sharp increase in the size of the fields attracted to Leicestershire and other rail-linked hunting countries. It was not unusual for carriages, or complete trains, to be hired to transport followers and their hunters. For the hiring of a train in those days was as easy as borrowing a vehicle from Rent-a-Van today.

A memorable day in 1880 was the Kirby Gate meet attended by the Rev. Jack Russell, of terrier fame, who travelled all the way from Devonshire to see Tom Firr hunt hounds. Parson John was then eighty-four and one of the most honoured hunting personalities in England. His terriers were almost as famous as the Belvoir hounds. But he and Tom Firr might be pardoned a wry smile if they could see some of the animals that still bear Russell's name. Parson John's curiosity about Firr had been aroused in conversation with Colonel Jack Anstruther Thomson, Tom's former Master with the Pytchley, who was a great friend of the sporting cleric. J.A.T. had taken his beagles to hunt the Devonshire hares when he was stationed at Exeter as a young officer, and that was how he first met Jack Russell.

The visit of Jack Russell was just one of the numerous journeys by celebrities to see Tom Firr hunt on the Melton side. Yet, if his diary entries are anything to go by, he obtained just as much fun from the other side of the Quorn country, with only local personalities present.

"Saturday, Feb. 24th, 1883. Hathern Turn. A splendid day's sport. There was a small field out, amongst them being Mr. Coupland, Master Duncan Coupland, Mrs. and Miss

Brooks, of Whatton; Lord Belper and Miss Strutt, Mr. and Mrs. E. H. Warner, Lord Ferrers, Miss Tidmas, Messrs. C. Martin, J. D. Cradock, A. Martin, H. Storey, Pares, Col. Chippendale, Messrs. Robson, Briggs, Wells, Tidmas, James, Bolesworth, Harriman etc.—

"Oakley Wood our first draw, and here we found a remarkably stout fox. The covert was nearly drawn blank, but in the very last bit of it old *Dewdrop*'s husky voice told us one was at home and, after two turns round, he went away by Shepshed Mill and on to Garendon, crossing the park. Then through Booth Wood and on to Dishley, over the Loughborough Steeplechase Course, and swam the canal at the back of the stand. Thence to Loughborough Big Meadow, before reaching which an ugly brook crossed our path, which I got over all right, followed only, I think, by Miss Strutt, Miss Brooks, Mrs. Brooks and Lord Belper.

"Hounds swam the Soar, under Stanford village, and then went on at a much slower pace over the ploughs to Lewes's covert, by Rempstone and on to Costock. The pace over these ploughs was now very slow, and continued so until we got again on the grass by Thorpe in the Glebe, when it increased, and we ran merrily on by Mr. Warner's covert, then towards Wysall; but, bearing to the right, we soon reached Widmerpool village and crossed to the Square Plantings, after which hounds bore more to the right, and pointed for Willoughby. Just short of the mill they turned again, to the left. I could frequently see our fox a field or so in front, and the pace was terrific at this time. After crossing the Old Fosse Road, and just before reaching Curate's Gorse (The Curate), they rolled him over, bang in the open.

"Time altogether: 2 hours 25 minutes.

"Distance: as the crow flies 12 miles. As they ran 17."

THE BEST SEASON ON RECORD

There was little outward sign of the troubled situation which marked the closing stages of Mr. Coupland's reign. Awkwardly sited railway lines and the introduction of wire were inconveniences everyone could see. Another, less obvious, was an increase in the number of pheasant shoots, with at least two landowners in the area using former fox coverts as homes for gamebirds. A decrease in the number of foxes aggravated matters, and there was no doubt many of the missing foxes met their end in gamekeepers' traps, or had eaten poisoned bait. Yet all these problems were small compared to the threat hanging over the Quorn from another quarter — the dwindling financial resources of the Master.

Mr. Coupland had taken the Quorn to new heights, aided by Tom Firr, but he could not justify for much longer the large amounts of cash he was spending on the hunting country when his shipping business was facing collapse.

In that period a Master's outgoings were very heavy, for his expenses included the payment of compensation for poultry and damages. Most hunting men, unfamiliar with business, assumed that because the Master owned ships he must be exceedingly rich. They did not realise how large a part credit played. Mr. Coupland did not have a great amount of capital and was hard pressed when a slump in shipping reduced the volume of freight. He tendered his resignation in 1881 to a committee for the first time not presided over by Lord Wilton, who for sixty years had been the power behind the throne of Meltonia. (Lord Wilton died in March 1882, aged 82, soon to be followed by the other pillar of the Quorn, General Burnaby of Baggrave).

58

Figure 5.2   Jack Russell, who visited Tom

Sir Frederick Fowke, of Lowesby, pointed out that a large sum was owed to the Master on the Covert Fund; that they must raise £4,500 a year, and that they had no hope of the young Duke of Portland paying up for them, as some had hoped. No obvious, and willing, replacement for Mr. Coupland was available, but he was not the type of man to leave the Quorn in the lurch.

He struggled on for another couple of years, which were among the hardest his huntsman experienced. Tom Firr did his best to economise and to go as well on fewer, and worse, horses. It seems incredible, therefore, that part of this period in the Quorn's affairs was eulogised by Brooksby as *The Best Season on Record*. He describes the opening day as follows:

N Monday, November 5th, the season was, according to time-honoured custom, formally inaugurated at Kirby Gate. As with our birthdays, each recurring occasion brings a less sense of self-congratulation than the one before. Not that each opening meet is not in itself a welcome event—but there is the afterthought that another item has been entered against our very limited credit, and the account cannot go on for ever. Never mind—"Chal'k it up! Chal'k it up!" Mynheer of the scythe and hourglass. Rip Van Winkle never troubled himself about his score—nor recked the leap of Time. Why should we?

By coincidence, Tom Firr ended his 1883 — 84 diary with the words, "So ends the best season I ever saw."

Lord Lonsdale's name makes its first appearance in Firr's diary that season, when the sporting earl took his hounds to Scraptoft, by invitation, and clashed with Sir Bache Cunard's in Launde Wood. Count Kinsky "got an awful fall" over the Hoby raspers and, on another day, Tom himself fell heavily, "being brought home in Mr. Halston's dogcart."

Brooksby, in his inimitable style, described one of the marvellous January days when the Quorn ran a six-and-a-half miles point in forty-three minutes in the morning; and in the afternoon ran for an hour without an absolute check. "Both runs carried them far over the border into the Duke's territory; and both took them at great pace and over much beautiful ground." The full account was published in The Best Season on Record.

"Ye gods, how they fly!" exclaimed Brooksby. "The mottled pack, now running in a broad mass, is skimming up the second grass field in front; we are crowding through a gateway, into a rough meadow that is built for anything but rapid galloping." At one stage in the run Captain Doggie Smith and Alfred Brocklehurst landed together into a roadway, "Firr joining them at the same instant as if from the clouds; for certainly no other man could have made up the ground within fifteen minutes of extricating himself from the gorse, fully fifty people being then between him and hounds. The little brown is almost burst by the effort; but, very shortly afterwards, Mr. Coupland snatches an opportunity to change horses — setting his huntsman on the grey — while a moment's breathing time easily enables the blown one to bring the Master to the end of the run." Down to Holwell ironstone railway track they went. There was hardly a slackening of pace until: "The pack runs the waggonway for half a mile; most of us run it a mile, and join the bridle-road throng from Wartnaby, Kettleby and Holwell. But Mr. Cochrane carries out the principle; of *seniores priores* by boring a way through the over-hanging bullfinch alongside — and carries out also the huntsman and a grateful following from the trammels of the waggonway — though he bears an honourable scar on his cheek for the rest of the day, perhaps for the rest of the week." On to Clawson Thorns and another rail track. "It has been my fate to write of hunting for some fifteen years — and I aver, in sorrow and in truth, that the word *railway* is at the end of my pen at least fifteen times oftener now than when I was first entered to ink," lamented Brooksby.

"An old man fumbles willingly at the padlocked gates by his farmside; Firr rides lucklessly down to another pair of white gates some fifty yards away, where there is not even a pair of clumsy, willing hands with a key — while in anguish of soul he marks bold and bedraggled Reynard toiling up the next field, hounds a hundred yards behind him, and a flock of sheep scuttling between. Who shall say that a huntsman's career is without its agony?" The fox found safety in the main earths at Goadby Gorse.

Brooksby was then near the end of his career as a correspondent. But he never lost his bubbling enthusiasm, as can be seen from the following extract: "Over the hillside from Scraptoft, High Leicestershire, were pretty grass fields with some twenty men racing over them in blinding sunlight — hounds glancing in sight only now and then like flying fish in the air. The very acme of a Leicestershire burst is — it always seems to me — when hounds go a little quicker than you can, yet where there is free space for every man and every horse to be doing his best, irrespective of others right and left, or even in front. We don't see this every day. Either scent or country is generally lacking. But it is very

Figure 5.3 The new railway once more (near Twyford)

delightful when it comes — and then, and then only, does a good hunter seem to be at his best."

★   ★   ★

PORTLAND SAVES THE DAY

The end of the Coupland era came in 1884. Some money, but not enough, had been contributed after the Master pointed out that he could not go on paying the poultry and damage claims out of his own pocket. A continued slump in freights made his departure inevitable. He had been in office for fourteen years and was featured in an anonymous verse:

> Here's Coupland the Master, so natty and neat,
> So courteous his tone and so faultless his seat
> You would swear that our Coupland as Master was born
> All booted and spurred at the head of the Quorn.

But the natty Mr. Coupland was no longer at the head of the Quorn. Not only that — he put his hounds and his horses up for sale. The Quorn was facing a crisis again and the well-heeled followers did not seem in any hurry to save it; after all most of them could go out with the Pytchley, the Belvoir, or the Cottesmore. At the final sale, twenty-five horses fetched £2,200. It has been truly stated that horses, no matter how good, do not make a hunt. Only good hounds can do that, and the Quorn hounds were very special, having been brought to perfection by years of loving care from Tom Firr. He was deeply upset at the prospect of losing the pack, and for the first time since he arrived as huntsman at Quorndon he considered applying for a post outside Leicestershire.

The Duke of Portland, and other sources, indicated that Firr was at that time in line for the position of huntsman to the Royal Buckhounds, the most exalted post open to a professional. A house in Windsor Park and a Civil List pension went with the job. Others have put the date of that particular episode as two years later, when the Leicester Mercury referred to a rumour that Goodall was to resign the Windsor post and would be succeeded by Tom Firr. The 1887 report might well have been a recurrence of the earlier rumour, and the Duke of Portland was in a position to know the facts.

Whether it was the Buckhounds or not, Tom was certainly unhappy about the resignation of Mr. Coupland and made it plain he could not stay as huntsman without a first-class pack of hounds. He pointed out to the Earl of Wilton (the former Lord Grey de Wilton) that it would take eight to ten years to build up a pack from drafts and cast-offs. Tom was in a quandary. He was turned forty and was witnessing the disintegration of everything for which he had worked for twelve years. The Quorn without Tom Firr was unthinkable. Yet still the committee hesitated.

A high price was asked for the pack — £3,300, which was believed to be a record — but for twelve years the hounds had swept all before them, in the field and on the flags. Lord Wilton promised to do something about it, and he was as good as his word. He talked the matter over with the Duke of Portland, one of the leading heavyweights, and with Mr. Julius Behrens, of Leeds, who kept a large stud at Melton, and the three men agreed to take equal shares in the pack.

Tom was not thoroughly convinced. He had to think of his growing family and their security. The Duke of Portland again came to the rescue with a promise to the huntsman of £50 a year — the difference between Tom's Quorn income and the sum he could expect from the Queen's Buckhounds. Eventually the Quorn pack became the property of the country, and once more the Duke of Portland played a major role, presenting his share to the committee in gratitude for the seasons he had spent with the Quorn and Tom Firr.

Mr. Coupland was one of the best Masters the Quorn ever had. He was firm and just, a fine rider, a good field master and he ran the Hunt on business lines. But the nub of his success was in choosing the best huntsman in England and leaving him to get on with the job, in and out of kennels. The years with Mr. Coupland were among the happiest of Tom's life. His Master treated him as an honoured colleague and it says much for Tom's character that he never became loud-mouthed or bumptious. To mark their parting, Mr. Coupland gave to Tom a silver cup, which he left to his son, Frank Firr.

★   ★   ★

CRICKET AND CONCERTS

Into the breach caused by Mr. Coupland's retirement stepped Lord Manners, who offered to keep the pack going for a couple of years until someone else could be found. John Manners-Sutton, 3rd Baron Manners, was a popular figure, especially since his remarkable feat in winning the 1882 Grand National in a blinding rainstorm on his own horse, *Seaman*. The following year another Quornite, Count Kinsky, won the National on *Zoedone*, completing something of a Quorn treble, for it was just ten years after *Pathfinder* had won. Lord Manners was fortunate in having the benefit of an efficient committee, under the chairmanship of Sir Frederick Fowke. There was a guaranteed subscription of £2,500, with a covert fund, managed by the committee, of £1,500.

The new Master, aged 28 and a captain in the Grenadier Guards, had ridden several seasons with Tom Firr and wisely copied Mr. Coupland's good example in leaving the huntsman to his own devices as much as possible. Judging by the correspondents' reports and the gossip, a stranger might have been forgiven if he believed the Quorn had only one employee. In fact several good huntsmen emerged from the twenty-three whippers-in who were engaged by the Hunt when Tom Firr was there. One of these, for four seasons, was George Gillson (Cottesmore), grandfather of the Warwickshire huntsman of the same name. (The elder Gillson was also Frank Freeman's father-in-law).

Among the others were Will Capell, William Webb and Edward Haynes. There was another, who joined in 1881 as second whipper-in and stayed for seventeen years and who became almost another arm to Tom Firr: the indefatigable Fred Earp. And if Lord Manners had done nothing else, he would be remembered for his foresight in promoting Earp to first whipper-in.

Christened Alfred, but always known as Fred, Earp was a model whipper-in, seldom seen and never heard after hounds went away. Even the huntsman may not realise how much the whipper-in contributes to the success of a hunt, but let him make the least mistake and it is obvious to everyone. Fred was in that valuable circle of Hunt servants who make marvellous whippers-in yet do not have the extra qualities which produce a top notch huntsman.

Figure 5.4 Count C. Kinsky on *Zoedone*

When Fred Earp went to the Quorn they had probably the best pack of hounds in England, nearly all home bred, and Fred was a good choice to handle them. He became inured to such comments as, "Firr went like a bird. I never saw such a cast as he made to kill that second fox, and no whip in sight to help him. I don't know why Fred is brought out, for all the use he is." Perhaps only the huntsman saw that cap on the skyline, guiding the galloping cast to success in the failing light.

Such partnerships as that of Firr and Earp are not common, for outstanding first whippers-in do not go short of inducements to move elsewhere. As a huntsman Fred could have had a house, prestige and all the extra emoluments and perks, to say nothing of the sovereigns which strangers were expected to give, before "capping" became official practice in the Shires.

★ ★ ★

By the time Lord Manners took over, Tom Firr was an established Quorn institution, not only as the huntsman but also as a leading figure in the civil and social organisations of the area. There were no tiers of local government spreading their blankets of authority over people's lives. Local affairs were in the hands of the Court of Quarter Session, the multifarious boards and guardians. Tom became a director of the Quorn Gasworks and of the Quorn Village Hall, a Guardian of the Poor, and a churchwarden. Late in his life he also purchased half a dozen cottages in the village.

During the Mastership of Mr. Coupland an annual dinner in honour of Tom Firr was instituted by Major-General E. S. Burnaby and held at his home, Baggrave Hall. They were sparkling occasions. At one of them the guests included the general's cousin, Colonel Fred Burnaby[1]; Captain Boycott (after whose name the phrase "to boycott" was coined); Captain Hartopp, Mr. Coupland and Harry Custance, the jockey. "Chicken" Hartopp brewed the punch, stirring it with a fox's brush.

The meet the next day was at Baggrave and Tom was invited to stay the night. The room where he slept had windows covered by shutters and thick curtains, so that it remained dark inside even when the sun was well up. This, combined with the late hour at which he had gone to bed, induced Tom to sleep on. His daughter, Evelyn, to whom he told the story, said, "His horror was great when an elderly manservant walked into the room and, drawing the curtains back, remarked, 'It's a fine hunting morning, sir, and the hounds are waiting for you on the lawns.'"

In the summers of his youth Tom had an interest which took second place only to hunting. From May to August, when his duties allowed, he was to be seen on the cricket fields of Leicestershire. He captained the Quorn House team in the 1880s, generally making top score and taking a wicket or two as a change bowler. And he was said to have an eye like a hawk for a skied ball. Most villages had greens on which local teams competed until harvest time. There were also opportunities for promising players to join in country house matches with squires' sons and their friends. Although Leicestershire

---

[1]Colonel Fred Burnaby, who lived at Somerby Hall, became a national hero after a daring 370 miles ride from Kazala to Khiva in 1875, "to see what the Russians were about." He was killed by an Arab spear in 1885, during the Sudan campaign. Captain Edward "Chicken" Hartopp, of Dalby Hall, was an uncle of Mrs. Cessy Burns Hartopp, whose husband became Master of the Quorn.

Figure 5.5   Colonel F. G. Burnaby

did not qualify as a first class side until 1894, there had long been a strong cricket tradition in the county. Tom was a young hunt servant in Berkshire when Leicestershire's twenty-two beat the all-England team by an innings.

When he reached Quorn, Tom found that cricket was enjoying tremendous popularity and in 1878 he was one of the 13,000 spectators who saw Leicestershire take on Murdoch's Australians, with Bannerman and Spofforth (a match that the Australians won). Tom also visited the county grounds of Derby and Nottingham. The mighty W. G. Grace — seven years younger than Tom and a hunting man himself — was to be seen and the Leicestershire stalwarts included the bowlers Bobby Rylott and Dick Pougher and the pugnacious C. E. deTrafford, who captained the side to first class status.

The Firrs' family life was happy. Tom was proud of his children: John, Frank, Gertrude, Tom Freeman, Evelyn, William, Charles, Florence and Grace. But they knew little of their father's life outside the home because Tom was very reserved and did not discuss his work with them, nor did he say much about the people he met. The children, in the Victorian way, were not allowed to ask questions. Almost the only insight they had of his world of hunting was when he returned too tired to write his diary and dictated an account of the day's events to one of the girls. He drank in moderation, claret, whisky, or sometimes a pint of ale, but his favourite drink when he arrived home was a cup of tea.

Tom, with his fine voice and commanding presence, was in demand for the village

Figure 5.6 Colonel Burnaby's country house, Somerby Hall

concerts and suppers, which were so much a part of country life. He did not play the piano and contented himself with singing the songs he had composed. His children remembered how the villagers clapped and shouted, "Tally-ho!" whenever their father walked on to a village concert platform. Tom's eldest daughter, Gertrude — who married Vincent Dearden, well known as an organist and conductor in Leicester — usually accompanied her father on the piano.

A staunch Conservative and monarchist, Tom could make a good speech at political meetings, many of which he addressed in the cause of the Manners of Belvoir and Mr. Clowes, the former Master of the Quorn, for whom Tom had whipped in. (Disraeli had become Prime Minister for his second term in the year before Tom became the Quorn's huntsman and was to stay in office for nine years).

The many facets of Tom's character and his ability to master most pursuits no doubt helped him in his job. He was a skilful artist, as his sketches of Quorn Alfred and other hounds bear witness. He also excelled in the gentlemen's sports of shooting and fishing, and he could play a reasonable game of billiards.

Tom's reputation was further enhanced by the hunting articles he wrote for The County Gentleman and local newspapers. And he was selected by Lord Suffolk and Berkshire to contribute a section on the fox to the Encyclopaedia of Sport.

None of Tom's sons followed in his footsteps as a huntsman, but some of his descendants inherited a love of horses and hounds. Denis Aldridge, former secretary of the Quorn and of the South Atherstone, once employed Tom's nephew, Percy Firr, as a groom. The sight of Percy on a horse gave the older members quite a start, for he was the image of his illustrious uncle.

The children followed their father in other ways. John became a veterinary surgeon. Thomas, who qualified as an engineer, went to Nyasaland, captained a cricket team at Zomba for several years, and on his retirement to Quorn became a member of the Loughborough Cricket Club and secretary of a local golf club. All four daughters loved music. Florence was also an ardent worker for the Church and taught in the Sunday School; Evelyn found a sporting outlet in golf and became a leading player; Grace (Mrs. Lambert) was a proficient actress; Gertrude (Mrs. Dearden) was a talented pianist.

PRAISE FOR LORD MANNERS

Sport was not of the best in Lord Manners's first season, but that was through no fault of the Master. Bad scenting conditions were general; Tom Firr was out of action for a time, and late in the season he reported, "My horse, *Nap*, dropped his legs into the ditch and unfortunately broke his back."

There was, however, an unusual run that season, when the Quorn and Belvoir combined at Flint Hill and killed their fox after another hour and ten minutes, Frank Gillard, as the senior, hunting the joint packs. Harry Bonner, the Belvoir second whipper-in, told Isaac Bell about it and his account was published in Bell's A Huntsman's Log Book. So many widely different versions of that incident have been recorded, but Bonner's story, as reported by Ikey Bell, is worth repeating as it is probably the least biased.

"Tom Firr arriving with his hounds at a gallop, slipped them into Flint Hill, and took up his position next to Bonner, telling him to 'get on.' 'We don't require *your* help, Mr.

Firr, to kill *our* fox,' said the nettled young whipper-in. At first Firr looked pretty sour, but suddenly he said in that charming speaking voice of his, 'No, Harry, but I require yours!' Bonner always says he regrets having been so hasty and to have answered back, when but a young whipper-in, the greatest huntsman of the day.

"The fox broke away; neither of them spoke; Bonner thought Firr had seen him, but on discovering he had not done so, charged through a rasping bullfinch out of covert and holloaed him away! After running a few fields, hounds checked in some foil. Firr and Gillard, who were riding side by side, pulled up, watching hounds making their own casts; a couple of Quorn bitches speaking to it. Gillard said to Firr, 'Tom, what are those couple?' 'They are the daughters of your *Weathergauge*, Frank.' Gillard cheered them, and, touching his horn, the two packs were hunting together once again."

Tom's 1885 diary reported a November day, from Hathern, "running from 11.30 to 4.45; hounds were stopped at the Monastery in the dark after a real sporting run ... Mr. Harriman alone was with me when I stopped hounds." On 21st December: "*Gratitude* got jumped on and broke her leg." And that year's diary ended with the statement: "The very worst season, as far as weather went, in the memory of man. Stopped twenty-eight days and many times hunted when it was no mean feat. Nearly all the time squalls of wind and rain were sufficient to make sport almost out of the question. Very bad scenting season nearly all the way through. Killed 29 brace and 19 brace went to ground in 51 days."

Lord Manners was an earnest young bachelor with his fair share of worldly goods when he accepted the Quorn. In the summer of 1885, however, he married and something had to go — he resigned the Mastership at the end of his second season. Despite the shortness of his term in office, Lord Manners was a popular Master. And he left a monument, the Adam's Gorse covert, which he enclosed and replanted. One other noteworthy event of Lord Manners's time was the appointment of Otho Paget as correspondent to The Field, in succession to Brooksby. The younger son of a younger son, Otho Paget was always short of money. But he kept a pack of hounds ($12\frac{1}{2}$ inch beagles) and hunted with the Quorn and the Cottesmore the other four days of the week for sixty years. He was second only to Brooksby as a hunting journalist and Tom Firr was lucky to have two such scribes to record his achievements.

★　★　★

Figure 6.1   The Third Lord Manners

CHAPTER 6

'WARE POISON!

When the committee came to discuss the possible successors to Lord Manners it did not take long for the name of Warner to come to the fore. The question was, which Warner? Mr. J. H. B. Warner was among the first to be considered. He was the eldest son of Mr. W. E. Warner, a successful hosiery manufacturer in Loughborough, who had bought Quorn Hall from Sir Richard Sutton's executors in 1855. The hall was inherited by Edward Warner, the second son. J. H. B. Warner had been prominent in the controversy about the division of the old Quorn country which strained many relationships beyond repair in the late 1870s, and he consistently refused to acknowledge Sir Bache Cunard's Hunt, always wearing "ratcatcher" when he went out with it. In the end the committee plumped for the youngest of the three Warner brothers, the more amiable Captain William P. Warner. He and J. H. B. Warner lived at Langton Hall, Market Harborough.

Guy Paget believed that the huntsman might have had something to do with the appointment. "One cannot help thinking that Tom Firr had a hand in it and pulled strings. Living for so long at the Quorn Hall Kennels, he must have come into almost daily contact with the Warners and have ridden home in the dusk many hundreds of miles, stirrup to stirrup."

New ideas were beginning to gust through the Quorn establishment and the appointment of Captain Warner, although not the obvious one, turned out to be a sound choice. He had strong support from Mr. William B. Paget, of South Fields, Loughborough, who explained to the Hunt committee the part he, in conjunction with Captain Warner, proposed to take in the management and expenses of the Hunt. Four years later he was to become joint Master with Captain Warner. Mr. Paget was descended from the Pagets of Ibstock, who kept harriers "for the amusement of their friends and neighbours" in the early eighteenth century. There is no record of the proposals he put to the committee, but action taken suggests the line he took.

Soon after Captain Warner accepted the Mastership, the committee gave twelve months' notice to Lord Ferrers to surrender the Donington country. When this became effective, Tom Firr could once again enjoy good hunts on the Charnwood Forest, and to the north of it. The fresh policy of the committee was a setback for the Meltonians. As Colin Ellis put it, "The centre of gravity (if not the centre of gaiety) was quietly shifted back from Melton to where it was in Meynell's time — to Quorn and Loughborough."

To understand the controversy, one needs to go back beyond the Coupland era to a period when the original Quorn country was divided into three. Mr. Coupland, in the central portion, had Mr. Tailby (Billesdon side), and Lord Ferrers (Donington side) on either hand. In 1878 Mr. Tailby announced his resignation and Mr. Coupland moved to take the Tailby country back under the Quorn's wing. But Mr. Tailby handed over to Sir Bache Cunard, who passed the country to Mr. Fernie, and the argument festered for years, eventually being resolved in 1920, when the Quorn recognised the Fernie Hunt. So all attempts to claim back the Billesdon country failed. The situation in regard to Lord Ferrers and the less attractive Donington country was, by contrast, straightforward. Despite the protests, the Quorn's right to take back that country was beyond doubt.

Captain Warner's appointment was not announced until a general meeting in April 1886. Another controversy arose at that meeting, not nearly so damaging as the Billesdon country affair, however. A grazier and cheese manufacturer, Thomas Nuttall, of the Manor House, Beeby, wrote to the committee on behalf of a meeting of farmers, saying that the farmers should be represented on the committee and should be consulted about the appointment of any Master of the Quorn. Fortunately, the diplomacy of William Paget prevented a nasty row. He discovered that a principal grievance was the non-settlement of poultry claims, about which he was able to reassure the owners. And four farmers, including Mr. Nuttall, were appointed to the committee.

Captain Warner's Mastership was an unqualified success. He bought in all Tom Firr's favourite horses at Lord Manners's sale and conducted the Hunt's affairs in a quiet, businesslike way, being greatly helped by Mr. Paget. The captain's first season was full of incident. Tom Firr's diary notes that on 11 October a fox "went to ground in a hole where there was a wasps' nest. I am afraid he would have had a bad time of it in there."

Monday 1 November 1886, Kirby Gate. ". . . tremendous crowd, looked like going to a large race meeting, all roads being lined. The sun was very hot indeed."

On 8 November at Lowesby, "Fred Earp fell in the park and had to be taken home in a dogcart."

Sport had been better on the Forest that season, and on 7 December Tom broke into verse:

> "For'ard on, for'ard on, there's a scent for a hundred,
> The big 'uns are racing away for a lead,
> A note from each throat is defiantly thundered
> And threatens outpacing the fastest brave steed.
> Come catch us who can, they seem to be calling,
> While fences in front look black and appalling."

FROST AND A FALL

A big frost stopped hounds from 14 December until the 24 January meet at Baggrave. After the six weeks' lay-off the going was doubtful and horses were kicking and squealing with freshness. The first draw was the Prince of Wales's covert, which held a good fox, but they had barely started before Tom's horse skated on a downhill slope and turned over on him. He reported, "Frost not out of ground. Had not gone three fields when I fell and broke my collar bone in two places and otherwise damaged, so that I was laid up for over six weeks. Hounds were stopped at Beeby and went home."

Tom was lucky to escape with a broken collar bone. He returned on 5 March, but had to lay up again for a week. When he resumed the horn on 21 March he soon accounted for three foxes. In Tom's absence Fred Earp had been hunting hounds. According to Guy Paget, Fred "failed to kill a fox fair and square. His bag was one chopped in covert, two killed against wire netting, two mangy ones, a three-legged one (Forest side), and a bad fox only ran in Nanpanton Gardens; one bolted and killed."

By the first week in April, Tom was back in form. "Went to the Trussels and found, and had a very good run, but unfortunately changed foxes. Nine-mile point to Ashwell (Oakham). Hounds came home by train."

Wire was becoming more of a nuisance and was testing the hardest nerve. Tom discovered that Sir Bache Cunard's country was seriously infected with the wire menace. That other impediment to hunting, the shoot, was never far away. "Up to this date we had not been allowed to go into Bradgate Park coverts on account of shooting," Tom observed on 7th February, 1888.

Foot followers also hampered many a potential run, and the coldest of weather did not deter them. "Scraptoft. Again very frosty. Still we hunted, and had a capital forty minutes' gallop with the boldest fox ever seen. Finding in the gorse, he dashed over the lane leading to the farm, and jumped the hedge out of it like a greyhound; then swung round to the right, and in the face of a hundred foot-people, whom he did not fear in the least. Went smack through them, and made his point. Going first up to Barkby Thorpe, he afterwards ran round by the foxholes (Hungarton), by Keyham. Leaving Scraptoft Gorse a little on the right hand, he raced on over the Uppingham turnpike to Thurnby Gorse, where the earths were open and he got to ground fifty yards in front of hounds."

An unusual day for the Hunt began when they found at Whatton Gorse a fox long resident in the covert, an animal known to local people as "the big 'un." It was Tom's first glimpse of that particular fox, who led hounds a merry dance to Oakley Wood, then doubling back to run alongside the Soar towards Kegworth, over a road and in a wide circle until they caught up with him in a farmyard. Next they raised "a real black" one and killed him at Whatton after twenty-five minutes. The black fox was believed to be a descendant of some which were imported by the Russian ambassador in about 1815, and turned down in the Belvoir Woods.

Hounds outran everyone, including the huntsman, in a fine run from Crosby Spinney the following year. "I got a bad fall towards the end and was picked up by Fred, quite unconscious, and remained so for some time," said Tom. The pace of his hounds was entirely to Tom's credit. He did not believe in heaviness and he would not sacrifice essentials for Belvoir tan, or sharpness for bone. Yet he notched up another championship in 1890, with Quorn *Dreamer* by Rufford *Galliard*. That was the year Captain Warner's old friend and neighbour, William Paget, became joint Master and presumably increased his share in the expenses and management to a fifty-fifty basis.

That year also saw the death of Tom Firr's horse, *Revolving Light*, after a "grand day" and, according to Tom, "entirely, I think, through lack of condition." Saddened, he went home and wrote:

TOM FIRR

"Over pasture or ploughland he'd jauntily sail,
He loved to be in the first flight.
He'd skim the tall binder and lop the high rail,
At the brook in the valley he'd never turn tail.
When others were going, oh! why should he fail,
The gallant *Revolving Light*."

Lady Augusta Fane took part in that run, on her brilliant hunter *Yellowhammer*, after hounds found in the Prince of Wales's covert, Baggrave Park. "Only those who jumped the rails in the park ever saw them again," she said. The outstanding part of the run was a thirty minutes burst. Hounds had raced away. Another view was given by Otho Paget: "It was very seldom that Firr did not get to the head of affairs in the first field, however badly he might have been placed at the start." They appeared to change foxes in Tomlin's Spinney, before Firr reached them, so that the pace continued undiminished. *Revolving Light*, brother of a Grand National winner, *Gamecock*, had been bought by Captain Warner at Lord Manners's sale. "Firr must have asked too much of his mount in the early stages of the run, and, being unable to get a second horse, was never able to give him a breather," said Otho Paget.

In April 1891 occurred what Tom called "the most deplorable day ever known" and which emphasised the impact of gamekeeping and poisons on the Quorn country. Starting from Quorn Wood, many coverts were drawn blank and Tom decided to trot off to Thurcaston Gorse. "While crossing the park (Bradgate), the keeper holloa'd from the hill beside Old John. He had seen a fox, no doubt a bagman. Hounds did not at first care to own the line, but settled to it at last and ran out of the Park towards Benscliffe, when a first class hound called *Truman* was seen to stiffen his limbs and fall and die.

"Hounds went to Hammercliffe, to Bawdon Hill, the run ending in a snowstorm. Here *Fearnaught* fell and died, the effect of poison picked up in Bradgate coverts. Both were stallions, three-year-old hounds." Tom did not mention any action being taken about the hounds' deaths, but Bradgate was seldom visited after that, for some years.

HUNTING ADVICE

At the end of the 1890-91 season, Tom noted: "Season a short one. More frost than for years. Many days hounds went out quite unfit to hunt, and there have been a great number of bad scenting days. But the wind was the most trouble."

Never one to press his advice on an unwilling audience, Tom was always prepared to give the benefit of his experience when asked, particularly if his counsel were sought by the young entry. After a slow run, with bad scent, Tom wrote down his advice to beginners, which I feel is worth giving in full: "To some a hunt of this kind would probably be looked upon as small — I mean those who go in for riding for riding's sake, to whom nothing short of a quick twenty minutes over a big country can be looked upon with the least enjoyment. And this shows plainly the necessity of learning to love hunting in youth, or the chances are it never may come to you until the days of intrepidity are past and gone, and the sere and yellow leaf commences to make its unwelcome appearance.

"To be unable to enjoy a 'hunting' run means many days lost. Scent, that most peculiar of all things, will far too frequently prevent the fast gallops coming off, and admit of nothing else but slow and careful hunting; for, without a scent, it is impossible for hounds to run.

"If there should be any young gentlemen home from school for their Christmas holidays, who take an interest in the noble pastime, and should by any chance come across these notes, let them, until better information be received, ponder over them. Learn to love hunting in all its branches. Watch patiently the splendid work done by hounds on a bad scenting day, the manner in which they 'fling' themselves in their casts, making all points good with the least possible loss of time; trying every smeuse (hole) in the hedgerow when dashing down beside it, or picking out the line, bit by bit, finally wearing him down.

"On days of this kind, of which you will see many, hounds require lots of room. They must not be hurried or driven over the line, or your own sport will be spoiled. But this will come natural to you if you will only keep your eye upon them, which is at all times necessary, for your own enjoyment as well as for that of others. The hard-riding part of the business is sure to come to you if you have the pluck of the ordinary Englishman. But if you go in for riding, and riding alone, disappointment upon many occasions is bound to be yours.

"By speaking thus, I don't mean to say you must not look upon a quick burst as enjoyable. I think myself there is nothing so soul-stirring and delightful as to see hounds dash into the scent and drive along with that tremendous determination which speaks for itself. You have to 'ride', or you will see them no more. But these are exhilarating bursts, which do not fall to our lot every day. What I have attempted is to prepare you for the general run of enjoyment on any day's hunting."

★   ★   ★

THE MIDNIGHT STEEPLECHASE

It has been said that there can be no true perfection in art. Firr and Earp were as near to perfect as you can get in the artistry and performance of their craft. But they *did* blunder occasionally. Lionel Edwards, the artist, was talking with Earp when the whipper-in admitted he had once holloa'd hounds on to a red squirrel. It happened during an autumn day on the Forest side, while the bracken was up. Fred saw a flash of red along a wall that surrounded a covert. It looked so much like a fox's brush that Fred holloa'd on the hounds, which were close to him — and away went the squirrel. Firr came thundering up and said nothing when he realised Fred had made a mistake. Fortunately, hounds did not hit off a line.

Another anecdote, told by Charlie McNeill, concerns a mistake by Tom Firr, this time involving a rabbit. "I remember after a very good gallop, hounds checked just above Lowesby. Firr, after holding hounds well round forward, could make nothing of it, and, as it was late, nearly everyone turned for home. But one old bitch was standing waving her stern at a drain under a gateway. Tom Firr said, 'Fred, jump off and see if you can see through.' 'Yes,' said Fred, 'he's here all right. I can see his eyes!' So Firr told him to pull an old rail out of the fence and poke him out. This he did, and away up the side of the fence went an old buck rabbit, with the whole pack in full cry. I need not say Firr was furious. But it was his own fault. When Fred said he could see the fox's eyes, Firr had got off, who-whooped, and got the whole pack baying. So naturally they were over-keyed up. I rode back to Quorn with Firr that evening, as I nearly always did, and I have never seen a more miserable man."

Mr. McNeill saw an exceptionally good hunt in the Saturday country, during the Warner-Paget partnership, on a teeming wet day. His story illustrates the cunning a fox can display in attempting to disguise a scent.

"Nearly everyone left when hounds ran into Whatton Gorse. T. Firr asked me to go to the top corner. Hounds were running hard in covert. I saw a very tired fox come out and walk across to a large muck heap with urine all round it. He walked along, feet in the urine, and rubbed his back against the side of the muck heap, and then turned round and rubbed his other side in the same way. Then he slowly walked out into the field and downed himself in a lot of bent grass. Hounds came out lower down, apparently on a fresh fox, but I raised my hat and Firr stopped them and galloped up to me. Where did he go? I told him, and alas the end was soon over. It was the most sagacious thing I ever imagined a fox would do."

A "run" that Tom missed was the Midnight Steeplechase, organised by Quornites to celebrate Lady Augusta Fane's birthday. She claimed that she got into Tom Firr's bad books because she did not invite him to take part, but Captain Warner had asked her not to tell the huntsman anything about it, for fear he might compete and have an accident. "He reproached me, saying sadly, 'My lady, that was a bit of fun I should have enjoyed'."

It was to have been the Moonlight Steeplechase but the night of the full moon turned out to be overcast. Not to be outdone, the riders borrowed lamps and a van from the nearby railway station and fixed the lights to poles at each side of the fences. The men put nightshirts over their red coats, but one of them, Algy Burnaby, struggled into one of Lady Augusta's pink gossamer nighties. Most of the Melton population appeared to have gathered by the time the race started, soon after 11.30pm. All the spectators could see of the riders were flashes of white and pink as they passed the lights on the mile-and-a-half out and back again. Algy Burnaby won, although Otho Paget maintained that the prize would have been his but for the fact that the master of ceremonies changed the site of the winning post without telling him.

Reference to Lady Augusta brings to mind the increase in the number of ladies who hunted with the Quorn in the last two decades of the 19th century. At one time it was thought quite risqué for a woman to be seen on horseback and those who actually went to a meet were, in some quarters, regarded with disdain. Whyte-Melville referred to "two or three" ladies being at a meet in 1861, but by 1877 Brooksby was reporting that there were about thirty in a field of three hundred. Some of the ladies were very fine riders, and they needed to be for in a number of respects they had a more difficult time than the men. Not only did they have to ride side-saddle but custom decreed they should wear costumes which were positive death traps in a fall. It was not until the 1880s that a form of "safety skirt" was adopted generally, which came off at the waist and remained attached to the saddle when the rider was thrown. Improvements to the side-saddle and, later on, the introduction of aprons, also eased the situation. Queen Victoria gave impetus to the trend of riding for pleasure, and the Empress of Austria — who hunted with the Quorn, the Pytchley, the Cheshire and the Meath — helped to make riding to hounds a fashionable sport for ladies. However, it was not until 1891 that ladies were asked to subscribe.

Figure 6.2   The Empress of Austria — regular follower of the Quorn

TOM FIRR

A BAR AND A BARRISTER

William Paget, at fifty-four, was a fine looking man with a beard that was already white when he became joint Master of the Quorn. He and Captain Warner kept the Hunt running smoothly in all departments. But their reluctance to be in the first flight led to dissatisfaction among the Meltonians. Things did not go with a proper swing, complained the young bloods, adding that the Masters were never up enough to prevent hounds from being overridden. Some of the ladies argued that the Masters did not give Tom Firr enough protection. They knew just the man to inject new life into the Hunt; a real flyer who had the money to turn out the Quorn in style, in short the young, free-spending, hard-riding Earl of Lonsdale.

The person most affected by such a radical change at the top was Tom Firr. He had become an institution; so much so that his name was often linked with the toast, "Fox-hunting." A graphic illustration of his self-composure and dignity was provided in that period by his defence evidence in an action for trespass and alleged damages of £500, brought by a dairy farmer called Willoughby. It was claimed that hounds had chased some cows, biting their udders and causing them to slip calves. The farmer's allegations were shown to be as exaggerated as was the claimed damages. First he had to prove trespass. The plaintiff said the damage was caused on 16 January, 1893. Captain Warner pointed out that a frost had set in on 23 December and lasted until 23 January. However, he admitted that hounds crossed the farmer's field on the latter date, although he saw no cows.

Tom Firr then gave evidence. He was superb. He entered the box and bowed like an ambassador to the bullying counsel's, "Now, my man."

"I am not aware that I am your servant, sir."

Tom handled counsel, who was already rattled, as if he were an excited, rude child of feeble intellect. No, they were not his dogs, they were the Quorn hounds. No, the Quorn hounds in his time had never chased a cow. Of course he could not say what happened when he was not there.

"You say you have known the Quorn hounds since 1872?"

"No, sir. I have said no such thing."

"I have it down here, 'I have been huntsman of the Quorn since 1872.' Do you deny that?"

"No, sir."

"Well, what do you mean, man?"

"I was whipper-in in 1863 to Mr. Goddard."

"What has that got to do with it?"

"That Mr. Goddard was then Mr. Clowes's huntsman."

"You were a whip, were you?"

"No, sir. A whipper-in."

"What's the difference, my man?"

"The same as between a bar and a barrister, sir."

(Loud and prolonged laughter in court).

Tom continued: "Hounds are not common dogs. They are well-bred, well-disciplined and have good manners and, if I may say so, better than some people."

"Better than mine?"

"That is not for me to say, sir. I have never seen you hunting.

"Dogs of all breeds always attack at the neck; foxes and wolves at the flank. I am sorry, I thought every educated person knew that, sir."

A verdict was given of £51 against Captain Warner and Tom Firr.

Tom's only other encounter with the law was much more pleasant, but again it demonstrates his standing. On a visit to London he met Mr. Justice Hawkins over lunch at The Mitre, where Johnson and Goldsmith took wine. The judge, in his memoirs, stated, ". . . And there sits, at my side, enjoying his chop, Tom Firr, described as the king of huntsmen; simple, respectful, and respected, whose name I will not omit from my list of celebrities, for he is as worthy of a place in my reminiscences as any M.F.H. you could meet."

Brooksby, who never tired of talking about the Quorn huntsman, once told Ikey Bell, "Tom Firr could tie on an evening white tie better than any man I ever knew!" And he coupled this tribute with the comment that no other huntsman moved his hounds so quickly "before him" as Tom. No mean achievements!

★ ★ ★

Figure 7.1   The Earl of Lonsdale — Master of the Quorn

82

CHAPTER 7

LORDY TAMES THE CAVALRY

In considering the ups and downs of the four seasons of Lord Lonsdale's Mastership of the Quorn and his relationship with Tom Firr it is more important than at any other time in this narrative to understand the backgrounds, motives and the personalities of the people involved.

Hugh, 5th Earl of Lonsdale was thirty–six when he took the Quorn on the resignations of Captain Warner and Mr. Paget. The titles, vast wealth and estates of the Lowther family, including a virtual kingdom in Cumbria, settled on him suddenly and unexpectedly.

When he was a child the chances of his ever succeeding to the earldom were so remote as not to merit a thought. He was the second son of a nephew of the 2nd Earl. Hugh's brother was only two years the elder. Yet within a space of ten years the 2nd Earl had died, and so had Hugh's father and brother, after each had inherited the title. Almost overnight the raffish, impecunious "Mr. Hugh" became "my lord," a powerful, sought-after personage with a seemingly bottomless purse, even though the strings were held by trustees.

Hugh was then only twenty-five years of age, with boundless energy and brimming with schemes for spending his fortune. And there were plenty of spongers and beautiful women to spur his ideas along. Because his hopes of attaining the title were so slim, he received no formal preparation for the responsibilities and his claim to have been "brought up in the stable" was not far from the truth, although he did go to Eton. The upshot was that he was a brilliant rider, with an enviable knowledge of horses, farming and the countryside and yet was completely ignorant of the various business enterprises on which his fortune was based.

At the age of nine he had come to notice by being in at the kill when the field had been reduced to four. Thereafter his ambition was not to become earl but to be Master of the Cottesmore, which had been the "family pack" of the Lowthers — or so it was claimed — an ambition he eventually achieved. Long before that pinnacle was reached he was Master of the Woodland Pytchley (1881—85), and during that period he bought the Blankney pack, establishing it at Brigstock.

Tom Firr was sixteen years older than Lord Lonsdale. As we have seen, he was kennel born and bred and had been the revered huntsman to the Quorn for twenty-one years when the new Master arrived in 1893. Tom was strong-willed and dignified, with firmly implanted views on hounds and hunting methods gained in a lifetime of experience. He *was* the Quorn.

Brooksby said in a letter to The Field on Firr's retirement, "He has been to the hunting world what Dr. Grace has been to the cricketing world — the Champion." A similar analogy was used much later by Lady Oxford and Asquith, who, as young Margot Tennant, had hunted with Firr. Lamenting the "mediocrity" of the post-Edwardians, she wrote, "There are no outstanding British figures like Fred Archer, the jockey, Arthur Roberts, the comedian, Kate Vaughan, the dancer, Tom Firr, the huntsman, Worth, the dressmaker, or Grace, the cricketer."

That gives an indication of the respect and admiration lavished on Firr, which he accepted with calm self-assurance. Hugh Lonsdale, on the other hand, could be brash and impulsive; he was certainly colourful, he splashed his money around, he made dedicated friends and implacable enemies, and in many ways he was ahead of his time. He chose yellow for his carriages and servants' livery, an idiosyncrasy — together with the colour of his hair — that earned him the affectionate nickname, "The Yellow Earl."

Clearly, Lord Lonsdale and Tom Firr were poles apart in their private lives. It was not just a question of station. Hugh had no children and led a profligate existence. Tom was a family man, quietly spoken and serious. Hugh's garrulous, boastful approach concealed a basic shyness and insecurity. Tom had a marvellous voice. Hugh strained his voice in childhood and made use of a silver whistle when hunting. That situation, however, was not unknown to Tom because his old friend and former Master of the Pytchley, Colonel Anstruther Thomson, also used a whistle.

Two such personalities as Lonsdale and Firr were bound to clash, despite the high regard which they had for each other's ability in the hunting field. It must have been quite a jolt for Lord Lonsdale to arrive at a meet as Master of the Quorn and to find the field not looking at him but at his huntsman, whose word and signals were law.

Brooksby, paying a return visit to the Quorn, was taken aback when he saw the changes wrought by the new Master and his money. "No insignificant item in the scene (as may be imagined) was Tom Firr. Coming, as I did, a pilgrim to a hallowed land, I may be pardoned if I gazed with some curiosity upon a familiar face in a new setting. Relevantly or otherwise, the idea now given me was that of an old picture hung in a new frame — a *chef d'oeuvre* by an old master, redecorated and hung in an exhibition of works by new masters. That Tom Firr fitted his framing goes without saying. But Tom Firr, leathered as to the legs, hung with swan-necked spur, crossed with a stirrup strap, and mounted (superbly mounted) on a hog-maned steeplechaser with a long tail, made up a total that to my mind would best be set down as Tom Firr *en aspic*. It is needless also to add that Tom Firr forgot his casement as readily as he ever ignores his swamping field directly hounds run, and directly business is about. Indeed business has ever been Firr's engrossing principle, and to this he owes half his incomparable success."

VISIT TO BADMINTON

Eye-witnesses of this event included Brooksby's successor, Otho Paget, who spoke in favour of Lord Lonsdale's innovations. "All those who had ever met the new Master expected to see men and horses turned out with that perfection of detail for which he had always been celebrated. They were not disappointed. The careless or slovenly men might say that the fit of a hunt servant's breeches would not help sport, but hunting is, in the main, supported by the goodwill of those who never ride, and if the chase is to retain its popularity with the general public, it is essential to make a good show. The Quorn is the premier pack, and it seems only right that the staff attending them should be rigged out in faultless style, as an example and pattern to the less distinguished and poorer hunts. Although I cannot claim to have been a shining example of neatness in the hunting field myself, I can admire and appreciate it when seen."

Farmers, too, appreciated the control which Lord Lonsdale exerted over the field and his readiness to apologise, and compensate, for damage and inconvenience. Scornful references to the "Quorn cavalry" were not without foundation, as many of the first flighters had been drilled in the Lancers.

Lord Lonsdale was credited with giving the sport a new lease of life through his innovations. Even Harry Houghton, the runner, did not escape his attentions. Harry had been with the Quorn for so many years he seemed as much a part of the landscape as Cream Gorse or Thorpe Trussels, with his terriers and faded, cast-off scarlet coat. Not until the arrival of Lord Lonsdale was Harry officially recognised. Then he was clad in pristine hunt livery and equipped with a patent Lonsdale combined pick and spade, rockets and all manner of devices guaranteed to eject the most stubborn fox from a drain. Eight of his terriers were bought by Lord Lonsdale from Charlie McNeill for £10 each, a high price, but then Mr. McNeill's terriers were the best.

The public loved "Lordy", with his nine-inch cigars and his dash and flamboyance that provided some relief from their humdrum lives. One of his notable feats was his challenge match with Lord Shrewsbury, which became a one-man race against the clock. It happened during Captain Warner's Mastership and when he next went out with the Quorn, Lord Lonsdale was, in Tom Firr's words, "congratulated on his wonderful riding and driving performance, doing twenty miles well under the hour."

An argument over the respective merits of trotting and galloping led to a £100 wager between the two peers for a race of twenty miles to be covered in five-mile stretches using four styles: four-in-hand, pair, single and postillion. Lord Shrewsbury, under pressure from his wife, withdrew, so Lord Lonsdale set off on his own and covered the course in fifty-five minutes thirty seconds, an incredible performance considering the state of the road.

Lord Lonsdale's arrival at Quorn was preceded by the hottest summer and the earliest harvest local people could remember. As a result, the ground was like concrete and hunting commenced later than usual. Even before the season proper began, Tom received a foretaste of life with the sporting earl, who made it clear from the start that *he* was not going to sit back and let the huntsman rule the roost. At the same time he was quick to display the magnanimous side of his nature. That October he took Firr with him to Badminton to stay with the Duke of Beaufort, one of the most highly-respected people connected with fox-hunting.

"Left Badminton at 3.30 and was in the house at 8.45. Not bad travelling," Tom recorded in his diary. "The Duke and Duchess were both very kind."

On this and other visits to Badminton they were accompanied by the full Lonsdale entourage. This gave rise to a story that the Duke of Beaufort saw emerging from a special train Lord Lonsdale's private orchestra, keepers, dogs, loaders, valets, ladies'

Figure 7.2 The Duke of Beaufort — host at Badminton

maids, grooms and horses and exclaimed:

> *"My dear Hugh, I'm sorry your gardener is ill."*
> *"Ill? What makes you think that?"*
> *"Well, I don't see him here!"*

It seemed as if Hugh Lonsdale had to keep on proving himself and his early life was punctuated by numerous exploits, such as his sparring bouts against the world champion, John L. Sullivan, and demonstrations of horsemanship. Perhaps the best known of Hugh's feats with the Quorn was the day when, following a line he had not taken for some time, he put his horse, *Mullach*, at a post and rail fence with a ditch on the other side. Only when he was too far committed to stop did he realise that another fence, topped with wire, had been built on the far side of the ditch. Hugh collected his horse and cleared the entire obstacle, jumping a length of thirty-three feet. Basil Nightingale painted an impression of the extraordinary leap. He also painted the famous portrait of Tom Firr on *Whitelegs* which gives a good indication of Tom's seat and the way he appeared to glide over the countryside.

It was rare for Lord Lonsdale to have a fall. Tommy Burns-Hartopp saw him take one purler, caused by a sheep darting in front of him. Another fall in the Monday country was attributed to a lady cannoning into his lordship. An example of his composure was given at Gartree Hill when he was handed a message after he had ridden up to hounds. His horse sat down in the middle of the pack, but Lord Lonsdale remained seated and continued to read, while gently telling the horse to behave. The horse rose like a trained circus animal, with its master still undisturbed in the saddle. On another occasion, he took Tom Firr out with the Warwickshire, in March 1893, and once again he did not miss a chance of astonishing the field. Sir Charles Mordaunt described how Lord Lonsdale jumped in and out of the East and West Junction Railway near Bishops Itchington, "a feat we had not, up to that time, seen performed."

His control of hounds and his pet dogs was no less remarkable. Cecil Aldin, the sporting artist and illustrator, who was proud of his own skill in handling dogs, admitted he had met his match when he stayed with Lord Lonsdale at Barleythorpe. Aldin, Master of the South Berks, was taken into the dining room by his host, who asked how many dogs did he think were in the room. There was no sign of any, Aldin replied, whereupon Lord Lonsdale gave a low whistle and six large dogs appeared alongside his chair, each one roused from his allotted place beneath some piece of furniture.

The sadness which clouded his private life, stemming from the ill-health of his wife and the fact that they could not have a family, probably encouraged Lord Lonsdale to cover all his activities with a showy facade. His services to sport and to the nation, such as the private battalions he raised to fight in the Boer War and the 1914-18 war, far outshone his faults. He hated to be second best at anything. When he came across someone like Tom Firr, a complete master of the art of hunting and with the experience to back up his opinions, then sparks had to fly.

MANY A SLIP

The first big difference of opinion between Lord Lonsdale and Tom Firr appears to have been about the hounds. It goes without saying that Tom was extremely proud of the pack.

Figure 7.3 Lord Lonsdale on *Mullach* leaping 33ft, 4ins. (Painting by Basil Nightingale)

Lord Lonsdale had other ideas and brought some of his hounds from Brigstock. According to a story told about their exchanges on the subject of hound breeding, Lord Lonsdale was expanding on the theme of the advantage of bigness and bone when Tom remarked, "Certainly, my lord, except on the Quorn country, where I have noticed they are too big to get through the fences and too heavy in the shoulders to jump them."

Charlie McNeill was in the kennels on a later occasion when the Master was extolling the virtues of hounds he had introduced to the Quorn. "I pointed to *Arrogant*, a big dog with one ear half white, very easy to recognise," Mr. McNeill recounted in a 1950 letter. "I said, 'That's a lovely dog.' 'Yes,' said Hugh Lonsdale, that's one of my Woodland Pytchley dogs.'" The quiet voice of Tom Firr stopped him, pointing out that the Master was mistaken. "Mr. McNeill means *Arrogant*. I won with him at Peterborough."

When Tom asked about the horses, he was told not to concern himself, because he would have the best of mounts. When he asked if he should order the men's clothes, as usual, from Rugby he was instructed to await the arrival of an outfitter from London. The "seven years peace" under Captain Warner and William Paget were over.

Never one to do things by halves, Lord Lonsdale chose the showpiece opening meet at Kirby Gate to put his stamp of authority on the Quorn, in front of thousands of spectators. It was like a Bank Holiday on Epsom Downs. Masses of people on foot and in carriages gathered to watch the first fox go away, according to tradition, from Gartree Hill. Contingents from Leicester, Oakham, Grantham, Loughborough, and even Derby, lined both sides of the Melton-Leicester road and their vehicles stretched back for a mile and a half.

The arrival at the meet was spectacular, the yellow carriages thundering up and his lordship cheerfully acknowledging the plaudits of the vast crowd.

Then, consternation, the Master ordered Tom Firr to avoid Gartree Hill and take hounds on the other side of the River Wreake, away from the spectators. Tom was aware of the repercussions that would have, not least among the non-riding farmers, but his advice was ignored. Lord Lonsdale offered a simple explanation — he knew that Mrs. Hartopp, whose family owned Gartree Hill, had died during the summer and he sought in this way to pay tribute to her. He had drawn the covert when cub-hunting, but that, of course, was very different from the brouhaha of an opening meet.

Miss Cessy Hartopp, who became the wife of a Master of the Quorn, Captain Burns-Hartopp, wrote down her own recollections of the event and her notes were passed to the present author.

"From time immemorial the Quorn Hounds had always drawn Gartree Hill covert after their opening meet at Kirby Gate on the first Monday in November," she wrote. "It was an event being looked forward to by everyone, of every standing, for miles around. Farmers, occupiers of land and cottagers and tradespeople all gave the day up to it, and asked relations and friends to join them. In fact the day was treated like a Bank Holiday.

"But on the first Monday in November 1893 the crowds waited and waited, and at last we all had to realise that they had gone elsewhere; and the great day was spoilt for all the holiday parties, as disappointment and indignation took the place of all the enjoyment which had been anticipated.

"That evening several of the tenants and other sufferers came to me and asked me to find out the reason why the years-old custom had been disregarded. I promised to write to Lord Lonsdale to ask this, and also to express deep disappointment and indignation. I

Figure 7-4 The Quorn's Beehive Kennels

did this and said I should be obliged if he would explain, and also if he would let me know *when* the covert would be drawn, so that I could tell the other local people.

"Lord Lonsdale replied that he had not drawn Gartree Hill as he thought I should prefer his not doing so, on account of my mother having died some months ago. But as she had died in early July and he had drawn the covert when cub-hunting since, it was not a very convincing reason. Also, if it *was* the reason, the kind thought would have been better carried out if he had let me *and* the general public know beforehand, so that they would not have suffered. I was not married at the time and I fancy that the fact that the protest was made by a *mere girl* was almost unbelievable."

No one considered the possibility that the flamboyant Earl of Lonsdale was too shy to ask an opinion or to consult Miss Hartopp. Another *faux pas* by Lord Lonsdale that day arose when some of the field moved off the road to give hounds a free passage to the unexpected draw. The Master, conscious of his promise to protect the farmers from damage, berated them for jumping on to a crop of rye. One of the number was the landowner, who said he knew the difference between rye and rice (flax) on his own land. In any case, it was an experimental crop which had failed and was due to be ploughed in.

Tom Firr, in his account, stuck to the facts and voiced no opinion. "A great crowd as usual, and no end of vehicles, well filled into the bargain. Gartree Hill was not drawn today. The order was given for Mr. Cartmell's Spinney. This was, however, drawn blank."

One from Welby osier beds went to ground. There followed a long, slow run from Saxelby Wood, at the end of which the fox went to ground in a drain on Mr. Coupland's farm at Six Hills. "Bolted him, and hounds quickly ran into him," reported Tom. "A very pretty twenty minutes from Walton Thorns to ground at Prestwold ended a nice day's sport."

The following day, Tom recorded "a moderate day's sport" from Woodhouse Eaves. Overnight, the huntsman was said to have offered his resignation to Lord Lonsdale, but to have withdrawn it in the morning, after the Master arrived with a "man to man" apology. That is perfectly consistent with Hugh Lonsdale's mercurial character. He could flare up in an instant, and lash out at those nearby with fist or whip. Just as quickly he would become contrite.

TOWN MEET ATTRACTS 12,000

Towards the end of that eventful month Tom noted a run over country which is now almost completely covered by roads and buildings. From Swithland, they found in Mr. Frank Paget's Gorse and ran by Birstall. Hounds swam the Soar, went on to Birstall Bridge and crossed the Midland Railway to Barkby Thorpe, then running fast to Scraptoft, over the road towards Thurnby, turning right at the brook. Then to Humberstone and got to ground in Mr. Tertius Paget's Round Spinney, the site of which is now near the middle of Leicester.

When hounds met in Loughborough Market Place for the first time in years, people from miles around poured into town to see them. "There never were so many people seen in Loughborough before — supposed to have been about 12,000," said Tom. "The weather, being like midsummer, just suited them. The Mayor, Alderman Cartwright, gave a lunch in the Town Hall, and everything went off well — but for the day's sport, which was a bad one."

The Quorn, to rub in their superiority against the Pytchley "white collar boys," easily won a six-a-side point to point from Hickling to Wartnaby Hill, after a challenge from the Pytchley. "This was a good business and caused great cheering," Tom commented. Among the Quorn six was Count Zbrowski. The count, during a run with the Quorn, jumped both gates in and out of the Great Northern Railway, within two fields of Lord Morton's Gorse. The six-barred gates were each five feet high. The count's horse hit the second gate with all four legs, but he got over without a fall. He was killed while racing his Mercedes car near Nice in 1903. Always in the first flight at the big fences, he introduced the red ribbon into Leicestershire as the sign of a kicker.

The *esprit de corps* continued to wear thin in other areas, however. Lady Augusta Fane praised Lord Lonsdale as one of the very best horsemen in England; she admired his management, but pointed out that the field did not like to be dragooned and treated like children. She added: "Lord Lonsdale had another maddening trick of interfering with his huntsman when hounds came to a check, and invariably declared hounds were in the line of a hare — and ordered them to be cast back, which often ruined a good run."

Lady Augusta — who was a bridesmaid at Lord and Lady Lonsdale's wedding — said there was a sigh of relief when, in the absence of Lord Lonsdale, his brother, Lancelot Lowther, was deputed field master. "How everyone, including the huntsman, enjoyed themselves." Lancelot, who succeeded to the title on his brother's death, was a different personality altogether. With him, Tom Firr was able to organise the day to his own, and the field's, liking.

Hugh Lonsdale, however, wanted to hunt hounds himself. He solved his problem by purchasing the Brocklesby dog-pack and hunted it on bye-days on the Forest. Otho Paget had a day or two with Lord Lonsdale and said he saw some good sport, but he added, "in my opinion the hounds were too big for an enclosed country where the hedges were thick. It prevented the pack from carrying a good head and getting quickly together."

CHAPTER 8

A TERRIBLE BLOW

Despite his lavish expenditure and his seeming indifference to his sources of supply, Lord Lonsdale liked to have value for his money. And when the trustees of his estate expressed concern about his prodigal spending, he attempted to recoup some of the cash from those followers who wore the Hunt button yet avoided a just payment for their sport. The £3,700 in subscriptions hardly met the kennel expenses, to say nothing of the stables. There were often five hundred people out on a Friday, but few of them were inclined to tender subscriptions on the scale demanded by the new regime. Lord Lonsdale devised an easy way of identifying, and perhaps shaming, those who were wearing the Hunt button without subscribing. He ordered a new Hunt button to be made by one supplier, to whom he gave the names of those who had paid their subscriptions and were thus entitled to wear it. Again he neglected to consult anyone or to explain his idea. And the design of the button, with a large coronet — the mark of a peer's private pack — was regarded as an insult. There was a minor rebellion against the wearing of the button, but Charlie McNeill, who hunted from Quorn throughout Lord Lonsdale's time, described as "absolute nonsense" a story that one or two men cut off their old buttons and wore safety pins instead.

A lengthy article in The Windsor Magazine during Lord Lonsdale's Mastership defended the Meltonians against accusations of snobbishness which had grown in the seventy-five years since the "inflated panegyrics" of the Quarterly reviewer, parodied by Surtees, gave rise to that reputation. Nobody at Melton worth thinking about cared very much what form a man's credentials took, so long as he proved himself a sportsman and conformed to the first principles of hunting with a subscription pack.

"He need not be like Lord Plymouth and Sir Francis Burdett, who each subscribed £400 a year to the Quorn Hunt, and he will not be ostracised though his means may limit him to less sport than others revel in." There were, however, obvious reasons why a man of slender resources should choose Leicester or Loughborough, rather than Melton, as his headquarters.

If he could manage to stay at Melton, "there he will find himself among the choicest spirits of his age — whatever that may mean — and if he can hold his own with them across any country within hacking distance north, south, east or west of Melton Mowbray, when Tom Firr, Frank Gillard, Charles Isaacs or George Gillson has got

93

Figure 8.1 Tom Firr with his beloved hounds

Figure 8.2   The Quorn Hunt Button

hounds away on the scent of a good fox, he will be as near the heights of perfect bliss as a human being can hope to reach in this world."

Explaining the attractions of hunting with the Quorn, the correspondent, Henry Pearse, went on, "It is a merit of the Quorn foxes in these days that they do not break at the same corner of a covert, nor make the same point so often that the line of their run almost to a field may be foretold directly they get away. Hereditary instinct does not take that form with them probably because none among their progenitors has beaten Tom Firr and the Quorn pack often enough to have fallen into the habit that is second nature. It is just as likely, therefore, that you may cross the glorious Vale of Twyford with a fox from Cream Gorse, Thorpe Trussels or Ashby Pastures, as with one from Gartree or Burrough Hill and all are coverts dear to the hearts of Meltonians."

A note of caution was added for the sportsman who might take the writer at his word and head straight for Melton. "One would need a good stud to hold his own with Lord Lonsdale and Tom Firr, even if the Quorn only came within reach of Melton twice or thrice a week; add the chance of a long run with the Cottesmore, Belvoir or Mr. Fernie's on other days and you will find that second horses for every day, and something in reserve to replace the lame ones, are essential for full enjoyment of all that fortune brings."

ROYAL VISITORS

On the subject of snobbishness, Lady Augusta told a story about some young men who played a practical joke on a friend because they thought he displayed "swank" in flying an extra-large Union Jack over his hunting box.

They took the flag down during the night and spread it on the ground outside Barkby Hall, where it was seen by more than three hundred people who turned up for the meet in the morning. The flag owner was so angry he missed seeing a famous run. The run, from Barkby Holt to ground in Stockerston Wood, covered twenty-six miles, according to Tom Firr's estimate, and, although it was over grass, not more than twenty-five of the three hundred were left at the finish.

All manner of intriguing characters inhabited the Shires in that period, and one of the most fascinating was the Earl of Harrington, who hunted the South Notts country, adjoining the Quorn, for thirty-five years. He was a law unto himself and would pop up in the most unlikely places with his white beard parted and blowing on either side of his face as he rode. One day, the last Monday of cub-hunting from a meet at Lodge on the Wold, the Quorn clashed with Lord Harrington's in Bunny Park and ran some way together before dividing, the earl going on with one lot and Tom Firr with the other. Both packs lost. They met again at Colston Bassett. "Our hounds were all there. The others were two couples short," reported Tom.

Denis Aldridge had a similar experience years later, when out with the Atherstone on the Charnwood Forest side. They bumped into another pack, apparently on the line of the same fox near Ratby Burrows; then out from the shadow of the trees came two eerie figures on horseback, one with a white beard whipping round his face and both of them in ancient, lengthy red coats. The Atherstone members recognised Lord Harrington and Fred Earp (who by that time had left the Quorn) and for about an hour the two packs hunted together.

★ ★ ★

Alan Pennington acted as field master in the absence of Lord Lonsdale for part of 1895, Tom reported, "his lordship being at Lowther entertaining the Emperor of Germany."

The Kaiser's love of sailing was said to have been a reason for Hugh Lonsdale keeping his late brother's yachts and frequenting Cowes, where Hugh and the emperor became friends. Quite a stir was caused in London and Berlin by Kaiser Wilhelm's acceptance of Lord Lonsdale's private invitation to visit Lowther Castle. The show Lord Lonsdale put on for his royal guest would have done credit to the Earl Marshal himself. Huge crowds lined the route and the emperor was borne to Lowther in a tremendous cavalcade.

Another royal visitor to Lowther, the King of Italy, put a further strain on the Lonsdale exchequer, even though the king was not entertained so lavishly as the German emperor. The Lonsdale trustees warned Hugh that the funds were running low and he must cut his expenditure. Towards the end of 1896 the secret was out — Lord Lonsdale had offered his resignation to the Quorn committee. This news landed like a bombshell among the farmers, who had benefitted greatly from Hugh's iron control of the Quorn field, and from his munificence. On 14 December the meet was at Beeby, and Tom Firr noted in his diary, "Before moving off, Mr. Nuttall presented a petition to Lord Lonsdale, asking him to continue the Mastership." This was the same Thomas Nuttall, of Beeby, who had led the campaign of ten years earlier for farmers to be represented on the Hunt committee. Every farmer in the Quorn country signed the petition.

As Douglas Sutherland, in his biography of Lord Lonsdale, pointed out, "It was a request he was no more capable of refusing than of cutting off his own right arm. He withdrew his resignation on the spot."

The episode provides yet another illustration of the "soft" side of Hugh Lonsdale's nature. Tom Firr saw more than most of the earl's difficult side, but he also knew the attractive qualities: his compelling charm, his long memory for a kindness, and his princely generosity. After he found that Tom was keen on shooting and fishing, Lord Lonsdale invited him for three years in succession to Lowther to shoot grouse and to fish.

Figure 8.3   George Gillson — famous Cottesmoor Huntsman

Tom's daughter, Miss Evelyn Firr, recalled that the whole family was taken on two of those visits. "We stayed at the Old Vicarage, in Askham village. We were all invited to join in a day's otter hunting and finished up for lunch in the open air, laid on a long table by Lake Haweswater." On the third occasion, Tom stayed at the castle for the grouse shooting.

Lord Lonsdale also took Tom with him to Ireland, for two or three days' hunting with the Meath, and they stayed with the M.F.H., Mr. John Watson. They were quite at home, for the country was nearly all pasture, with all types of fences and, as with the Quorn, Baily's recommended "the best horse bred."

Signs continued to indicate that Lord Lonsdale's resignation could not be delayed for much longer. He tried, by means of a circular letter, to attract more subscriptions. When that failed, he pushed through a proposal to adopt the Irish system of "capping" for non-subscribers. There was a pessimistic ring to Tom Firr's diary entry for the Thrussington meet on 17 February 1897: "Capping was commenced today, each stranger to pay a pound. I hardly think it will answer; at least no good will come of it."

The system lasted into the following year and was then dropped. But it was re-started in 1903 after a meeting of the neighbouring Hunts. The money went into the Damage and Poultry Fund, reported The Sketch. "If any man is mean enough to refuse, the collecting official will report to the Master, who will simply say, 'The gentleman must pay or go home; if he does not, I shall take hounds home.'"

Unfortunately — or perhaps fortunately so far as the "honest" members of the field

Figure 8.4 The Earl of Harrington

were concerned — it did not turn out to be as simple as that. Otho Paget had the unenviable task of prising the sovereigns from the strangers. "Let me say now that extracting those golden coins from the pockets of visitors was one of the most unpleasant tasks that has ever fallen my lot," he wrote. "With very few exceptions did they have the right amount ready to hand out, and the job of searching in a crowd of three hundred for strange faces lost me many chances of getting a start." Old friends returning for a day with the Quorn did not greet him with the warmth he expected. And some went out of the way to avoid him, and chortled if they succeeded.

A FRACTURED SKULL

The 1897-98 season began with no hint of the turmoil that was to overtake the Quorn before another year had elapsed. There was an excellent run in late November after one went to ground near Ratcliffe village and was evicted by the terriers. Scent was poor and the fox ran through Seagrave village. Firr persevered and eventually hounds killed the fox close to Ella's Gorse. On Monday, 27 December, the meet was at Brooksby. Hounds found in Ashby Pastures, making a slow start and then running fast from Ashby Folville, across Twyford Vale and on towards Little Dalby Hall, where they caught up with the fox.

Four days later occurred the accident that virtually ended Tom Firr's career. There is no better way to tell what happened than Tom's own words in the final entry in his diaries.

Figure 8.5 Tom Firr's grand-daughter, Mrs Grace Pickard with James Teacher (courtesy: Jim Meads)

"The last day of the old year brought with it a most excellent day's sport, but a terrible blow to myself. After drawing Shoby Scholes and Lord Aylesford's covert, we went on to Ella's Gorse, the first time this covert had been drawn this season, found, and went away towards Willoughby. There pointing for Curate's Gorse, and afterwards by Broughton Station and Old Dalby.

"A right hand turn took us by Dalby Lodges and Six Hills, by Mundy's Gorse and there on to Wymeswold, and killed him in Hoton New Covert. This had been a very fine run of forty-eight minutes, with a better scent than we had seen before during this season.

"We found next in Walton Thorns, a brace. Killed one, and went away with the other over a nice line, leaving Six Hills away on the right, and after about twenty minutes' good going somewhere on the right of Wymeswold, I unfortunately jumped a fence into a pit, and was completely knocked out, my skull being fractured! Was taken home in a carriage and, some weeks afterwards, went to Brighton for a month, which did me good. But I did not recover sufficiently to hunt again that season, except for one day."

CHAPTER 9

THE QUORN PAYS TRIBUTE

Tom never completely recovered from the fall and his weakened condition made him more aware of the sciatica, that bane of hunting men, which had troubled him for years.

Lord Lonsdale ended the 1897-98 season hunting hounds five to six days a week, with his brother, Lancelot Lowther, as Field Master. Towards the end of that season Colonel Anstruther Thomson saw Tom at a Barkby Holt meet and they rode home together to the kennels, for tea. Tom had a fur coat, which he offered to J.A.T.'s wife, saying it had been given to him by a lady. He had been too embarrassed to wear it, although he knew that "her ladyship" would be the first person to see him if he went to a meet without it. "Sure enough, it was her ladyship and she said, 'Why haven't you got your coat on, Tom?' I said, 'It's not cold enough, my lady.' She said it was *quite* cold enough. So next time I put it on, and I never felt so ashamed of myself in my life as I did that day riding through the village."

For some time Lord Lonsdale's agents had been sending him urgent reports about the decline of his Hodbarrow iron mines, where the seams were becoming worked out. In the summer of 1898 he was given no choice. The flow of iron ore, and cash, was down to a trickle and major economies were essential.

There could no longer be any question of him continuing as Master of the Quorn. He waited until the last moment before making his announcement, in the hope that something might turn up. Then came the poignant sale of his horses at Tattersall's. The Prince of Wales and the German emperor sent representatives to the sale, at which Lonsdale's eighty-four horses went for a total of 18,228 guineas. Afterwards he was too shattered to do anything except go home quietly for supper with his wife.

It is clear the Quorn committee realised the dilemma he was in, for no criticism of his resignation, or its timing, appears in the Hunt minute book, despite the harsh words directed from other quarters. Indeed, Lord Lonsdale continued as an active member of the committee in a period when new kennels were built and the pack was purchased. On the credit side, he left the next Master to inherit a firmly disciplined field. He had also kept most of the farmers happy, yet his generosity created some discontent. For example, at Christmas he sent the principal farmers a brace of pheasants each, a gesture that did as much harm as good, because jealousy ensued among those who were left out. This created problems for his successor.

Figure 9.1   Captain Burns-Hartopp — saved the Quorn from the Midas Touch

SAVED FROM THE MIDAS TOUCH

If medals for valour were awarded to fox-hunters then surely one would have been struck for the man who followed the Yellow Earl. Captain "Tommy" Burns-Hartopp knew precisely what he was letting himself in for. He sized up the odds, which were heavily loaded against his comparatively slender purse, and he went galloping in. He accepted the Mastership because, as he put it, he "loved hunting and loved the Quorn country." Colin Ellis put it another way: "It has been said of Captain Burns-Hartopp that no better man ever lived for getting a bad horse across a good country. Possibly the committee had this quality in mind when they pressed him to agree to hunt the country after Lord Lonsdale's resignation in June, 1898. If the Quorn Hunt was not exactly a bad horse it was a notoriously difficult one to ride."

In accepting the onerous duty, Captain Burns-Hartopp reversed a trend which was beginning to worry many people who loved fox-hunting. "There is no doubt that he not only saved the Quorn, but hunting all over England, from the touch of Midas," commented Guy Paget. "If Hartopp had failed, the golden rot might have set in and no one but a millionaire could have been an M.F.H. in the shires."

Tommy Burns-Hartopp did not fail. The enthusiasm and jovial appearance of the new, young Master were contagious. He was a large man, well over 6ft., and he had a beaming smile that seemed to envelop the field, putting everyone in the right mood for a good day out. His wife, Cessy, was equally popular. Her family had been Quornites for generations. All the gallant captain's vitality was needed to get him through that first season.

The portents had been fair: Tom Firr appeared to be on the mend and the Quorn's new secretary, Mr. G. Tempest Wade, was proving to be a tower of strength. An early blow was the confirmation by Fred Earp, the loyal first whipper-in, of his decision to go to Lord Harrington as kennel huntsman. Captain Burns-Hartopp appointed Tom Gabbitas as first whipper-in and Walter Keyte remained as second. As far as Tom Firr was concerned, the more easy-going nature of the fresh régime was a relief. Captain Burns-Hartopp sent him to Harrogate for convalescence and then to Waterville, Co. Kerry, to enjoy the salmon fishing.

When cub-hunting started the ground was like iron. Tom maintained that he had recovered, yet his family knew otherwise. They noticed his drowsiness on his return from hound exercise and a persistent irritability. Soon after the start of cub-hunting the end of Tom's career was put beyond doubt by a fall on the Forest side. He told Captain Burns-Hartopp there was a gap in a wall which he jumped, and his head hit a stone hidden in the grass when he fell. John de Lisle was at the scene of the accident in his grandfather's park of Garendon. Mr. de Lisle was feeling very proud, for he had just been told by the renowned huntsman that he could call him Tom, as the other gentlemen did. According to Mr. de Lisle, Tom fell as he was jumping out of Garendon spinnies. He seemed dazed, but remounted and jumped through a bullfinch. When the next man landed Tom was lying motionless. There was no sign of his horse having fallen, but the hard ground would probably not have shown the marks. Young de Lisle galloped back to the house and brought up the family barouche, into which Tom was lifted and taken home. Garendon Park had a bad reputation. In Frank Gillard's time a Quorn whipper-in called Onion was killed by a fall there when he chased after a white stag, which cannoned into Onion's horse.

Figure 9.2 The Presentation to Tom Firr on his retirement

104

Colonel Charles Rich — "The Old Crock," of *Horse and Hound* — saw Tom Firr jolted by a fall not long before the Garendon incident. It was on the Donington side, with substantial fences, which looked even more formidable because the leaves were still on and the ditches were difficult to see. "Tom Firr was just ahead of me when his horse put his feet into a really blind one and came down. I caught his horse and he said he was all right, but I did not like the look of him."

TESTIMONIAL FUND

It was obvious that Tom would not be fit in time for the opening meet at Kirby Gate. Still he did not give up the fight to get back in the saddle and to be with his hounds. The Master ordered him to Bournemouth for a period of rest and arranged for him to see a specialist. A sombre letter arrived from Tom at Christmas, telling Captain Burns-Hartopp that the specialist "gives but little encouragement to think of hunting this season. It is indeed a dreadful thing to think of at this time of the year."

Within months Tom had turned into a sick, elderly man, bent and frail. It was heartbreaking for his family, and for anyone who had seen him slip over the Leicestershire fields in his heyday. In February 1899, the Master had to inform Tom, as gently as possible, that he could never hunt hounds again. Tom was reluctant to leave the kennels and the pack which had been his pride and joy for twenty-seven years. Captain Burns-Hartopp had to be firm, and told him that, while there was only one Tom Firr, those who followed must be left to make their own mistakes and find their own way.

Sir Arthur Markham, M.P., who hunted from Baggrave, had once offered Tom £1,000 to write of his experiences with the Quorn. The huntsman replied that he was a riding rather than a writing man. Now that he had time on his hands, however, Tom tried to write his memoirs. He soon had to give up because his head ached so much.

The Prince of Wales's name headed the list of subscribers to a testimonial fund, which reached an unprecedented total of more than £3,000 for "the finest huntsman who ever blew a horn." In April 1899 several hundred people gathered on the lawn in front of Quorn Hall, close to the kennels, for the presentation. Lord Belper, chairman of the Hunt committee, handed Tom a cheque for £3,200 and a silver salver.

A contemporary account of the proceedings, by Otho Paget, stated: "There should be nothing sad in the acceptance of a handsome salver and a substantial cheque, but everyone felt it to be a painful occasion, and there were few who had not only a choky feeling in the throat before the ceremony came to an end. The man we have idolised as a huntsman, and who has served us for so many years was sitting there before us, his health completely wrecked in showing us sport. Little more than a year ago he was riding as brilliantly as ever and now, by an unfortunate accident, he is cut off from following the profession that had become part of his life. We acknowledge him to have been a king amongst huntsmen and now, at this moment, we feel the inadequacy of the tribute we pay."

After Firr retired he found some consolation in the company of Charlie McNeill, who became Master of the North Cotswold and of the Grafton. The two men first met when Mr. McNeill, as a young man fresh from ranching in Canada, took the job of secretary and sub-agent at Quorn Hall and was always to be found in the kennels. They spent many a happy hour with Mr. McNeill's beagles and when he took the North Cotswold in 1901,

Figure 9.3   Tom Firr's grave in the Quorn village churchyard

106

Mr. McNeill asked Tom to stay for part of the season at Broadway, Worcestershire, to give the benefit of his advice. Tom's visit to Broadway and the long talks he had with Mr. McNeill — one of the finest amateur huntsmen — acted as a tonic. Yet by that time Tom knew he had not long to live. It is doubly tragic that, for someone who had such a remarkable voice as Tom Firr, the eventual cause of his death was cancer of the throat. He faced death with the same dignified courage he had shown all his life. Once he had accepted the inevitable, his temper became milder and he seemed at peace.

Many of the Quorn first flighters and two of Tom's sons were serving in the Boer War. Tom lived long enough to know the war had ended and his sons were safe. He deteriorated rapidly in December 1902. An operation was performed, but his condition continued to worsen and he died the following night. The Quorn, and not a few other people, abandoned hunting on the day of Tom Firr's funeral. He was laid in the quiet graveyard at Quorn, just to the east of the church, within sound of the hounds.

★   ★   ★

107

Figure 10.1 A sheet of Tom's music

CHAPTER 10

THE SONGS
OF
TOM FIRR

THE SONGS OF TOM FIRR

Tom Firr's songs and verses delighted audiences in the Shires and beyond for more than twenty-five years. No Hunt supper or village concert was complete without a "turn" from the Quorn huntsman. It was harmless fun in an age when the country people had to make their own entertainment. All of Tom's compositions were based on incidents he had witnessed. They often expressed his innermost feelings. The verses about the deaths of hounds and horses spring to mind in this context. As for the songs, most of them started as straightforward rhymes, for which he composed airs, and some were set to accompaniments by Dr. C. H. Briggs, of Loughborough. Tom's eldest daughter, Gertrude, was a talented pianist and usually accompanied her father. Of course, Tom's ranking as the leading huntsman in England and his fine voice were tremendous advantages. Yet even when read "cold," without the atmosphere of hunting horns and red coats and rousing choruses, Tom's verses rattle along at a fair pace and are strongly evocative of sporting country life in Victorian times.

THE BIG 'UN

There lived at Whatton Gorse by fame
A fox well known to some by name,
Though not through slenderness of frame.
His many friends just round about
Thought sport he'd show, he was so stout,
But when hounds came — he was out,
Was the big 'un.

Those friends he'd treat with some abuse,
For once we heard a tongue let loose
Some words about a favourite goose.
Cunning dodger though was he,
A mistake made eventually,
The result of which could not agree
With the big 'un.

Maybe he'd not the fixture read,
Or a debauched night he'd led,
P'raps kept him sleeping in his bed
That fatal morn, when by surprise
His friends the pack bade him to rise
And shake the dust out from his eyes,
'Twas the big 'un.

Helter-skelter, away he went,
For Oakley Woods he first seemed bent,
Till met, and back for Hathern sent.
The runner in his coat of red
Now holloa'd fit to raise the dead,
And waved his cap above his head
At the big 'un.

Skimming o'er the pastures wide
That lay along the riverside;
On for Kegworth fast we ride.
The music, too, is quite sublime
Which issues from those throats canine,
They seem to say, "Today we dine
Off the big 'un."

They turn, but still keep up the pace
As on towards Lockington they race —
It might have been a steeplechase —
Till Reynard's bolt seemed nearly shot
As nearer to his brush they got;
For, take my word, they made it hot
For the big 'un.

While strength would last, he had to fly,
Until "Enough," he seemed to cry,
And turned for home, sweet home, to die.
Now baying round his lengthy form,
Now of his brush and pads he's shorn,
Now into a thousand tatters torn,
Is the big 'un.

THE QUORN HOUNDS

Hurrah! hurrah! what a glorious thaw,
Said I, to myself said I,
The frost and the snow must be quickly awa',
Said I, to myself, said I;
The Yankees again in their tips are all wrong,
They declared this frost would last many weeks long,
But we'll mount in the morn and join the glad throng,
Said I, to myself said I.

Awfully grand, as we jog to the meet,
Said I, to myself said I.
Each fox-hunting friend so warmly we'll greet,
Said I, to myself said I.
As he snorts in his mettle and jumps with pride,
As along the greensward we joyfully glide,
No worse for his rest is the steed that I ride,
Said I, to myself said I.

"Tally-ho," hark! hark! Oh! heavenly sound,
Said I, to myself said I,
No music compares with the note of the hound,
Said I, to myself said I.
Through the brake or bramble and brushwood they crash,
To the cry like shots together all clash,
There's nothing can equal the foxhound for dash,
Said I, to myself said I.

How they swing and turn and race for the lead,
Said I, to myself said I,
It is "bellows to mend" with many a steed,
Said I, to myself said I.
There's the parson in black so hard to beat,
Still keeping his place with hands, nerve, and seat,
With such a good man I can't hope to compete,
Said I, to myself said I.

For an hour or more they run and they race,
Said I, to myself said I.
I'm lucky indeed if I have a good place,
Said I, to myself said I.
Like the truest of Britons I'll do my best,
When pluck and energy come to the test,
And endeavour to hold my own with the rest,
Said I, to myself said I.

111

TOM FIRR

REFLECTIONS OF AN OLD FOX

As old pug lay curled in a dreamy snooze
With his pads tucked in and his brush round his nose,
Said he, "On this sedge I can snugly repose;
To me it's a bedding of down O', down O'
Down O', to me it's a bedding of down O'.

Thoughts of atrociousness trouble him not
When after his rounds back to quarters he's got,
'Tis sleep of the soundest that falls to his lot
Whilst curled in his bedding of down O', down O' etc.

Till the huntsman's voice rings loudly and clear,
"Yoic, over my beauties, have at him in there."
"Ah, ah," says old pug, "I'm awake to a cheer.
"That's the note of my friend, William Brown O', Brown O'," etc.

One shake and away he goes, stealing along,
And over the open he leads the gay throng,
Who find to their cost that the fences are strong
As one and another comes down O', down O' etc.

Says pug, "My dear friends, many lives are at stake
Whilst tracing my tracks o'er the line that I take.
My skin might be torn; you've bones that might break.
Is there pleasure in tumbling down O', down O' ? etc."

Yet to own we exist through sport I am bound;
Without it not one of our race would be found.
May each sportsman's heart and purse remain sound
And foxhunting never go down O', down O' etc.

IS IT TRUE THAT OLD FREEHOLDER'S DEAD?

Freeholder, the pride of the stable —
Freeholder, the gem of the stud;
To win at a show he was able,
Or race knee and hock-deep in mud.
His fences he'd all of them fly;
Over water no matter how wide,
Let timber be ever so high,
He took all as they came in his stride.
Yes, often the way to the front
Over Leicester's green pastures he's led.
But alas! he's no more in the hunt,
For they tell me the old horse is dead.
Large-hearted and deep in the chest,
Which enabled him ever to stay,
In all runs he was one of the best,
Be the distance or pace what it may.
He'd quarters as strong as a house,
On legs like iron he stood,
He'd a coat as sleek as a mouse,
And veins overflowing with blood;
He'd shoulders thrown into his back,
Lean neck, and grand snake-like head.
Never happy but when with the pack.
Is it true that the old horse is dead?
There's a time for all things they do say —
A time for to rise and to fall.
The strongest must some time give way,
For Time puts an end to us all.
Yet, old friend, it seems hard to believe
Death could us thus early divide.
Never failing, that I can conceive
When I think of that last gallant ride.
Now I never go into my room
But with sorrow I hold down my head;
That hide on the chair casts a gloom —
Ah! sad proof the old horse is dead!

TOM FIRR

TRYING TO DO A DEAL

(Written after hearing a covert-side conversation, 1890)

He's a fine little hunter, you bet.
In fact, he's as good as they make 'em;
In his stride all fences he'll get,
Where'er you may wish to take 'em.
Bounds off just in the right place,
Away in the next field he lands, sir.
And gallop, my word! Such a pace —
As fast as e'er man clapped his hands, sir.

Bill Tompkins can tell you a tale,
How I pounded the field at a yawner,
A hedge and a ditch and a rail,
Stuck high on a bank in a corner.
I was out with the _____ in a run
From Highwood they checked not a minute,
O'er the valley like demons they spun
Only me and another was "in it."

How's he bred? Why, old *Topthorn*'s his sire.
Believe me, there never was better.
His dam? Ah, my word, what a flyer!
If you'd seen her, you'd never forget her.
Is she sound? Yes, sound as a bell:
Just throw your leg over and try him.
My stable's so full, I must sell,
Or double the price wouldn't buy him.

Written in Hunting Diary, 31 October 1881, after a most successful cub-hunting.

*T*o covert, brave sportsmen on, on and away.
*H*ark, hark to the cry of the hounds.
*E*ach one, in his musical note, seems to say

*Q*uick for'ard, my comrades, we mean it today,
*U*ntil the death holloa resounds!
*O*ne shake of his toilet, the bold but the sly
*R*eynard takes up the cue, and he sails
*N*ow to baffle and beat them, his hardest he'll try.

114

*H*ave at him, my beauties, as onward we fly
*O*ver hedges and ditches and rails,
*U*p hill, or down dale, through woodland, o'er rill
*N*o matter what comes in the line.
*D*o your best to be with 'em, your motto be still,
*S*traight forward to th' ending of time!

THE WATERLOO RUN
WITH THE PYTCHLEY

(From a meet at Arthingworth Hall, 2 February, 1866)

Yes, many good runs have I seen in my day,
Through woodland, o'er pasture and plough,
But none beats the one, I must candidly say,
Which I'll try to describe to you now.
Right well I remember the picturesque scene —
Dull, drizzling and damp was the morn.
No gayer assembly may ever have been
Than was seen on the Arthingworth lawn.
Though big was the field, yet their numbers were few
Who saw all the fun from the famed Waterloo.

Eventless the morning, no sign of a run
Worth calling by any such name;
A bad fox in covert persistently hung
For an hour or more, to his shame.
For over an hour he swung round and round,
Ere aught could induce him to go,
Then he managed to beat us, got safely to ground,
And in shelter we left him below.
Mid-day had fled; at a quarter to two
A good fox was found in the gorse Waterloo.

The voice of old Morris, though not very shrill
Would almost awaken the dead,
As he viewed him away climbing over the hill,
And brought up the pack to the head,
Hard-riding young bruisers now came with the bound,
Whose courage or dash never slacks,
Inspired by the musical note of each hound,
Went jigging away on their hacks.
And not until Langborough Wood was passed through
Was a fair start obtained from the famed Waterloo.

115

The spinney called Shipley, now being in front,
Past Clipstone they gallantly sped;
Grief here commenced at the top of the hunt,
When *Valeria*[1] pitched on her head.
Where the binders are strong and the bullfinch is brown,
Such tumbles are sure to occur;
But it's only an artist who, when he is down,
Can think of retrieving his spur.
O'er Oxendon pastures like pigeons they flew,
And onwards by Farndon from famed Waterloo.

A check by the road, and again for'ard on,
They stick to their business like clay,
No doubt entertained of the Truth of their song,
While a *Governess*[2] teaches the way.
I could name some of those who are in the first flight,
But their numbers are scanty, I fear:
Messrs. Nethercote, Fraser, and Topham, and White,
With a jockey[3] not far in the rear.
Past Lubbenham Manor still onward they flew
Like lightning, the beauties from famed Waterloo.

Disaster and grief is the word of the day,
As one and another come down;
Usurper,[4] with an extra five stone couldn't play,
The Master's again on his crown.
Some lucky ones now are let up at the bridge
Near Bowden, hounds pause on the plough;
Thence on once again over furrow and ridge
And *Flasher*[5] is leading them now.
As nearer and nearer to Langton we drew
The brook crossed our path from the famed Waterloo.

A wide open brook at this time of the day
Is a poser, as most will admit;
Catch hold of his bridle and show us the way,
Whilst down in the saddle you sit.
Catch hold of the bridle and shove him along,
And o'er the wide water you fly.
My boy, it's much easier said now than done,
Though many good men have a try;
Yet Custance came up with a rattle and flew,
Clearing all in his stride, from the famed Waterloo.

116

A pause and a swing, then for'ard they go,
Sticking well to a sheep-stained line,
Past Langton Caudle, and thence to Cranoe,
O'er a country that's truly sublime.
Though fences were strong, some bound, and some railed,
And few men still left in the fray,
The pack o'er the pastures now steadily sailed,
With a *Ferryman*[6] steering the way.
A loud cheer of praise from the Master it drew
For the Duke, as they ran from the famed Waterloo.

Past Glooston to Keythorpe they merrily led,
Scarce a check in their onward career;
Of many brave steeds they were now miles ahead,
Whilst others were far in the rear.
Now Keythorpe was near, 'twas the end of the run,
As far as I'd any concern,
And myself from the saddle I hurriedly flung,
Poor *Fresco*[7] was done to a turn;
But game as a pebble, staunch, gallant and true,
He'd played his part well from famed Waterloo.

Miles sixteen or more by the flight of the crow,
And twenty, perhaps, as they ran;
Had fairly been crossed, but still onward they go,
As if they had only began.
Alas for the field! which was fast growing less,
No longer left in by the score,
All beaten and blown, as they're bound to confess,
Save the Master and one or two more,
Who still to the pack are sticking like glue,
To finish the play from the famed Waterloo.

But every long lane has a turning, you know,
And runs they must all have an end;
Now past Slawston covert, yet onward they go
Where the banks of the deep Welland bend.
But the dark shades of evening are closing too fast,
Of light there is left but a ray;
Hounds near to Blaston are now stopped at last,
And a good fox has won him the day.
To him, then, we'll fill up a bumper or two,
And hurrah for more runs like the great Waterloo.

117

TOM FIRR

Notes:

[1]*Valeria* was the mare ridden by the Master, Col. Anstruther Thomson, at the start of the run. He lost a spur and stopped to pick it up.
[2]*Governess*, the hound that hit off the line.
[3]Harry Custance, champion light-weight jockey. Three times winner of The Derby.
[4]*Usurper*, taken by the Master from Dick Roake, who was five stones less weight, and fell at the first fence.
[5]*Flasher*, hound leading the pack.
[6]*Ferryman*, hound bred by the Duke of Beaufort.
[7]*Fresco*, ridden by Tom Firr as second whipper-in.

A BYE DAY WITH THE QUORN

My stud is nearly done up,
My sport must soon by spun up.
No such season have I seen
   Since the day that I was born;
For a stable full of screws
Must give a man the blues
When he thinks he's bound to lose
   A bye day with the Quorn.

Heaving sighs both long and deep,
At the member's card I peep,
Giving Brooksby as the meet
   On this grand hunting morn.
I'll have a good look round,
They must go if lame or sound,
For on joining I am bound,
   A bye day with the Quorn.

As along the road I jog
My nag goes with a nod,
'Till I reach the place of meeting,
   With the hounds upon the lawn.
Then he looks and gives a neigh,
And his lameness throws away;
Oh! at home he wouldn't stay
   On a bye day with the Quorn.

Orange gin my spirits healing,
To show there's no ill feeling
Ere I follow up my pets,
   The bitches and the horn.
'Tis a field composed for sport,
Few of Friday's medley sort;
No crowd from streets or court
   On a bye day with the Quorn.

There's Cream Gorse in the distance,
Which offers no resistance;
Full of foxes that will fly
   At the sounding of the horn.
With a pack that truly race
Each man now takes his place,
For his heart is in the chase
   On a bye day with the Quorn.

Say, can anything surpass
A gallop o'er the grass,
Hounds straining, horses racing,
   The coldest blood runs warm.
We charge each rasping double,
No fear, nor thought of trouble,
Oh! give me sixteen couple,
   And a bye day with the Quorn.

Then my day's sport being over,
And my spirits all in clover,
Feeling young, fresh, and happy
   As the day that I was born,
I order up a jumper,
And fill myself a thumper,
Drink hunting in a bumper,
   And a bye day with the Quorn.

THE COCKNEY SPORTSMAN*

*Tom wrote at least three versions of The Cockney Sportsman. This one was written out twice and was signed by him, as if he regarded it as the definitive version.

A sporting enthusiast! All will agree
The note of the horn and the sweet melody

TOM FIRR

From the musical pack is the chorus for me
Since the day I commenced as a sportsman.
In a very fine nag 'twas my luck to invest,
Whose great jumping powers I had put to the test,
'Twas then that I purchased a suit of the best,
A proper rig-out for a sportsman.

Chorus:
So I'll mount my brave steed and a hunting I'll go,
O'er the wide open fields where the green grasses grow,
Though the binders be strong and the rivulets flow,
I'll be in at the death, like a sportsman.

So anxious to have a great day in the shires,
I threw in my lot with the captains and squires,
Determined to shine as a flyer among flyers,
A regular cut-'em-down sportsman!
Next morning I mounted and rode to the meet,
And much was admired for my elegant seat.
I heard someone say, "That's a rum 'un to beat,
A regular, bold bruising sportsman!"

Chorus: So I'll mount, etc.

We found a fine fox and away we all went,
To be bang in the front was my firmest intent,
'Till at the first fence on my head I was sent,
Which crowned me at once a brave sportsman.
To pick up the pieces I still didn't fail,
But found to my grief, when again I set sail,
In my haste to remount I was facing his tail,
So they called me "a Cockney sportsman."

Chorus: So I'll mount etc.

I righted my seat and without much delay
Put spur to his side, and went sailing away,
The timbers were rattled like skittles in play
With the ever bold rush of this sportsman.
All now went well 'till we came to the brook,
Which didn't seem less as I took a long look,
But bound to be with 'em by hook or by crook,
I dashed at it like a true sportsman.

Chorus: So I'll mount etc.

120

I roused up my nag for an excellent spring,
To fly the great gulf like a bird on the wing,
But he stopped on the brink and shot me clean in,
Over head went this jolly good sportsman.
Though battered and bruised there is nothing I fear,
'Tis the sport that I love, and will still persevere
To be in at the death with loud ringing cheer,
Who-oop!
Like a true and jolly good sportsman!

Chorus: So I'll mount, etc.

THE QUORN, GT. DALBY, 1890

(Written after the death of one of his best bitches, killed by a train).

For an hour or more he led them a chase,
O'er the greenest of grass, and kept up the pace.
Though railroads and rivers, and villages too,
Came into the line, he ran them clean through.
Till beaten and blown, and stiff as a post,
Still game, he reluctantly gave up the ghost!

Now standing erect, when placed on his feet,
In death as in life, his heart seemed to beat.
The country resounded with brightest of sounds,
The horn and the holloa, the baying of hounds;
All there to rejoice, bar one of the best
And truest of workers any kennel possess'd!

Now mangled and torn, flattened out on the rail,
Ne'er before was she known to be at the tail.
May he hear that shrill note full many a time,
The note which she uttered when crushed on the line.
And the heart beat high to the tune of "Remorse,"
Of the man who was riding the cursed iron horse.

TOM FIRR

IRIS

(Written by Tom Firr when he was huntsman to the North Warwickshire and sung by him at the presentation to the then Capt. Anstruther Thomson of a portrait showing the captain on his favourite hunter, *Iris*. Tune: The Old English Gentleman.)

I'll sing you a song, a fine new song,
Made by a mad young pate,
Of one of the finest hunters
Of now the present date.
To see him o'er a country go
At such a dashing rate,
And some of his performances
To you I'll try and state.

Chorus: 'Tis that slashing horse called *Iris*,
                One of the present date.

He's second to none in England
Which all of you must know,
Either in the hunting field
Or at the hunters' show;
For instance at Peterborough
To touch him there was none,
And likewise at Wetherby
He was pronounced A.1.

Was that slashing horse called *Iris*,
One of the present date.

If you put him 'neath the Standard,
You'll find him sixteen two.
His superior in shape and make
I'm sure you never knew.
Just go from his head to his tail,
And down to the fetlock;
Put fifteen stone upon his back,
He's firm as any rock.

Is that slashing horse called *Iris*,
One of the present date.

To see him at the covert side,
So quiet does he stand,
And if he hears a hound speak
He'll give his bit a champ;

122

And when the pack have found their fox,
And settled on him steady,
No matter in what country,
To go he's always ready.

Is that slashing horse called *Iris*,
One of the present date.

Hark! there's a view halloo away,
Far, on the other side.
And now all you hard bruisers
You'll have a chance to ride;
But wait a bit, and let the hounds
Get fairly on the line,
And if you keep near "Wall-eye,"
It will take you all your time.

'Tis that slashing horse called *Iris*,
One of the present date.

And now along the grassy vale,
Like pigeons they do fly;
There's some timber in the corner,
And nearly five feet high.
"Now," says one, "the first who goes
Will come down with a crack!"
But he flies clean over like a bird,
With the Captain on his back.

Does that slashing horse called *Iris*,
One of the present date.

Still on they go like lightning,
There is no time to dwell;
The fences big — the country deep,
And the pace begins to tell.
In another twenty minutes,
A wager I will bet,
The cock-tails will begin to stop,
And the swells begin to fret,

At that slashing horse called *Iris*,
One of the present date.

TOM FIRR

But from scent to view they've raced him,
He can no longer wear.
Who-op! they've rolled him over,
And the Master, he is there.
Now here's success to Captain Thomson,
Wherever he may go,
His equal in the hunting field
We never more shall know

For he's the very best of sportsmen,
Of all at the present date.

HARK AWAY

'Tis the month of dull November we so gladly welcome round
To hear the merry music of the hunting horn and hound.
Like fairies gaily dancing, each steed is proudly prancing,
Whilst anxiously advancing to catch the cheery sound.
Hark away! Hark away!
From wood or dell we're glancing. Hark away!

When the fox has left the covert there's no sport beneath the sky
The joyous chase can equal, as o'er fence and fields we fly.
As onward we're careering, each brook or rail we're cheering
Little danger ever fearing, as we race up to the cry.
Hark away! Hark away!
To the front we're boldly steering. Hark away!

See the beauties sternly pressing, how they turn and how they swing,
Over ridge and furrow skimming, like pigeons on the wing.
Then like each fleeting swallow, we join and gladly follow,
Right forward to the holloa our hearts we freely fling.
Hark away! Hark away!
For'ard, for'ard to the holloa. Hark away!

Over plough or sheep stained pastures for the scent they lowly stoop,
Then darting off so keenly, like eagles in their swoop.
Each bullfinch now we're facing, with hackles up they're racing
To the death so madly chasing and we hear the loud "Who-oop."
Hark away! Hark away!
Then homeward bound we're pacing. Hark away!

124

THE SONGS OF TOM FIRR

Of all health-giving pleasure, there's nothing can surpass
The meeting at the covert side, the gallop o'er the grass.
Promote them and we'll never our ties of friendship sever
But unite them more than ever, so we'll toast it in a glass.
Hark away! Hark away!
May hunting flourish ever. Hark away!

A meet at Isley Walton, December 1887.
The run was from Langley New Wood.

"Go hark to the holloa; hark, hark to the holloa."
They've found, I declare, and the fox is away,
Hounds fairly bounding to the horn that is sounding.
To judge by their manner, they mean it today.

Towards Diseworth now speeding, and *Rival* yet leading
With half a field start, she out-rivals the rest.
But once on terms even, as my name's *not* Stephen,
They're so evenly balanced, there isn't a best.

Right-handed now swinging, like demons they're clinging
To the scent, as they fling themselves over the brow.
You must not lose a minute who wish to be in it,
For if e'er we were in for a "good thing," 'tis now.

Crash goes the binder, now that's a reminder,
There's strength in the hazel, although it looks dead.
But unlike Jack Horner, who sat in the corner,
This grey in the corner stands smack on his head.

But I've no intention the luckless to mention,
Or those who with fortune got best through the fray.
There's no help for falling, what e'er be our calling,
In this world at times, so at least the folks say.

'Tis a rivulet flowing, no man can help knowing,
With an eye to the front, where the willow tree grows.
Go straight and don't fear it, put steam on and clear it.
With rousing and squeezing, smack over he goes!

125

This brook, called the Belton, the great guns of Melton
Would wistfully long for and dash at with glee.
Like a fierce charge in battle, come down with a rattle,
For take-off and landing are sound as can be.

Still onward they're running, no chance for the cunning
To nick them at turns, as is frequently done;
Then homeward to dinner, as I'm a big sinner,
Perhaps swear that they've had the best of the fun.

Though hard to decipher, 'tis Oakley and Piper,
Those woods on the left and now within sight.
Thence One Barrow 'proaching, and may be encroaching,*
Yes, no, not if I've learnt the owner aright.

Where monks live at leisure (oh, where is their pleasure?),
We pass it and soon reach the Charnwood Lodge plain.
Our fox through the heather finds end to his tether;
One turn round the wood and he's down with the slain.

*Hounds ran smack in among a shooting party in One Barrow Wood and rather upset their drive.

The opening meet at Kirby Gate, November 1889

Come away my brave sportsmen, away.
'Tis weather as cheery as May.
We'll off to the meet, good friendship to greet,
And cluster around with the pack at our feet,
To welcome the opening day!

'Neath those coats of pinken array,
And habits so charming and gay,
Our steeds will embark with glee on a lark
By kicking their heels in old Kirby Park,
To welcome the opening day!

Now all troubles and cares must give way,
No matter what others may say,
As onward we ride with pleasure and pride
And follow the hounds to Gartree Hill side,
To welcome the opening day!

Of the hundreds, each seems to say,
Old friend, it is hard to portray
Any such fun 'twixt this and the sun
So heartily now we'll join in the run,
And welcome the opening day!

"Tally-ho!" I just heard someone say.
They've viewed him, a bet you may lay.
Best of all sounds is a chorus of hounds,
As each to the front so eagerly bounds,
To welcome the opening day!

"Hark-halloa!" he has now gone away,
So each one his own game must play.
Now to be smart and get a good start,
Then flatter yourself you've taken your part,
So far, on the opening day.

Another verse acted as a gentle reminder to some of the Quorn's followers.
December 1890.

It frequently happens that when a fox turns he does so after getting through a fence; if you jump the fence on either side of the pack you cross his line and do an immense deal of harm, which happened on the present occasion. As a reminder, I would put it in verse:

When approaching an obstacle, narrow or wide,
No matter how much you may be "on the ride,"
Take a pull at your bridle, and shorten your stride,
Till the pack settle down to the scent t'other side.

When frost stopped hunting, Tom turned his attention to skating. January 1891.

What an awful time we have had of it — six weeks and a day of idleness. If that won't make a man's hair turn another colour, what will? It is all very well to say, "Why don't you skate like other people?" Good fun, skating, I found it, so here's my experience of it, after waiting and watching, watching and waiting, till I could stand it no longer:

127

They call it splendid weather, as they toddle off together
With their skates slung round their shoulders, but to me it is a bore.
What to me is most annoying, there is youth and age enjoying,
For they seem to feel more jolly than they ever felt before.

I saw them going daily, so happy and so gaily,
Till I thought I'd like to join them, but I had no skates to wear;
At length becoming jaded, with the dullness that pervaded,
I at last became persuaded for to go and buy a pair.

"The Acme did you say, sir? 'Tis the proper skate today, sir;
No nasty straps to bother when attaching to the boot.
We can fit you to the letter, you cannot find a better,
'Tis the best the trade produces and I guarantee 'twill suit."

On the ice I gaily started, like a meteor I darted,
The outside edge I did it, and many stars I saw;
When, trying something bigger, I cut a pretty figure,
My heels came up, my head came down — and then there came a thaw!

And lucky for me the thaw did come. Talk about the dangers of fox-hunting, why they were not in it.

A run from Great Dalby, February 1891.

On a bright and sunny morning, Great Dalby the fixture,
Where half the wide world had turned up it would seem,
With ladies in number to brighten the picture,
That clustered around on the old village green.

How gay, too, the scene as its way slowly wended
Along the crook'd road to the famed Gartree Hill.
The mixture of scarlet and black nicely blended;
Oh, where is the eye that such charms couldn't fill?

Upon the next scene I will not dwell a minute,
To harbour such thoughts in one's mind isn't good;
Not worthy the name was a fox that was in it,
So onward at once to old Burrow Hill Wood.

Hounds hardly in covert when "tally-ho over"
Is heard in the riding, and then the gay crash
Of music struck up at the heels of the rover,
For the pack soon began to run with a dash.

THE SONGS OF TOM FIRR

"Hoik, for'ard away," it is now the great bustle
Takes place, for no words like these can impart
Such life into man, as he joins in the tussle,
Gets home in his beaver, and goes for a start.

The natural stand of the once famous racecourse,
Where many a pleasurable day has been spent;
The timber is rapped as we eagerly force
Our way to the pack, which now leftward has bent.

So soon left behind is the hamlet of Burrow,
And into the valley our part we must play;
While luck seems to have it, the wide ridge and furrow
Upon this occasion lies just the right way.

Steady my beauty, rather ugly that bottom,
Though not very deep or particularly wide.
The get-at is bad, the take-off is rotten,
The fence stands away on the bank t'other side.

Just dwell for a second, some other brave spirit
Will charge it as tho' 'twas a common sheep tray.
The odds they are great he will hit it and break it,
For you and for me he'll make easy the way.

Yet take we our chance if we come to a rasper
While the shrill notes scream loudly along on the breeze
The notes of those ladies, descendants of *Grasper*,
Which play to the tune, "Come along if you please."

O'er the best of the Cottesmore's wide open grasses,
The woodland of Owston is reached and run through.
Like shots from a gun, which so rapidly passes,
They were out t'other side, past Withcote they flew.

Some steadier hunting, and then to the holloa
Which is heard on ahead and just to the right
Of the coppice called Pryors; still onward we follow,
Then pass it and leave it behind out of sight.

Now on towards Preston our fox he is heading.
We sink in the hollow, we climb the next ridge;
The brooklet which through the next valley is spreading
We reach it and pass safely o'er by the bridge.

129

TOM FIRR

Some ten miles the point, tho' the line we have taken
Will add to the distance considerably; still
Our fox is ahead, we can't be mistaken
The ploughman is waving his hat on the hill.

Hounds now make a swing, the turn is left-handed,
And, pointing for Manton, right onward they lead
The way to its treacherous brook, which soon stranded
And brought to its depth more than one gallant steed.

But those who with luck haven't met with disaster
To the pack stick determinedly, up hill and down,
As they head for, and afterwards cross, Oakham Pasture,
Then make their approach very near to the town.

Again he is turning, his strength is fast failing.
Steady, you beauties, settle down, have a care.
Stick close to the line as onward you're sailing,
And the victory's yours, its glories you'll share.

Now back through the wood he had passed in the morning,
As before, like an arrow straight through it he flies.
The loud notes of the pack speak plainly the warning.
They race him, they chase him; in the open he dies.

Sporting verse was a popular pastime in the nineteenth century. Tom was by no means the only exponent. The following lines by another poet of The Chase — first published in *Baily's Magazine* — are included for their colourful descriptions of the Quorn field.

THE QUORN

The air was soft as a morning in May
As I mounted my hack, and I galloped away
By hall and by cottage, by meadow and lawn,
To Baggrave to ride and to hunt with the Quorn.

By Dalby, and Ashby, and Barsby I pass'd,
Till I reined up my palfrey at Baggrave at last;
And loud on the breeze came the notes of the horn
That was blown by Tom Firr as he rode with the Quorn

Of his skill in my lay 'twere presumptuous to sing,
Of horsemen the chief and of huntsmen the king;
So cheery his voice and so stirring his horn,
It would rise up the Pope to ride hard with the Quorn.

THE SONGS OF TOM FIRR

Here's Coupland, the Master, so natty and neat,
So courteous his tone and so faultless his seat,
You would swear that our Coupland as Master was born,
All booted and spurred, at the head of the Quorn.

Shall our host be forgotten whilst Inkerman's fame
Its halo still sheds around Burnaby's name?
Is he off to the wars? Will he leave us forlorn?
Ah, no, let him stay and ride hard with the Quorn.

The chase would be gloomy, the day would be sad,
Should we miss by the spinney the form of the "Lad."
And here is Lord Wilton, 'twere idle to warn
The gallant old earl not to ride with the Quorn.

And here's Little-Gilmour, though time, I declare,
Has wrinkled his forehead and silvered his hair,
Yet, keen as of old for the sound of the horn,
Long, long may he live to ride hard with the Quorn.

Ye ladies of Melton, I bid you rejoice
When you see at the covert the form of Tom Boyce,
Still handsome and gay as in manhood's first dawn,
He shines in the ballroom and shines with the Quorn.

The blood of the Douglas, so famous of yore,
Still shows to the front as so often before;
From the brows of the southron the laurels are torn
When Morton and "Shotie" are out with the Quorn.

And here's Grey de Wilton and fair Lady Grey,
Here's Pryor and Paynter to show us the way,
And Carington, too (who has taken the horn
Once carried by Lonsdale), is here with the Quorn.

"Doggie" Smith ever first on "Blue Ruin" is seen,
And Behrens the rich, and Samuda the keen,
Lord Wolverton, too, by Diana has sworn
Though swift are his bloodhounds he'll hunt with the Quorn.

All wild for a start on a flea-bitten grey,
Here's Tomkinson coming — get out of the way!
His steed in a lather, dishevelled and torn,
Let who will be last, he'll be first with the Quorn.

TOM FIRR

Here's "Sugar" the sweet, and here's "Chicken" the tall,
Here's Manners and Molyneux, Frewen and all.
Lady Florence is coming the meet to adorn,
Straight, skilful, and fearless she rides with the Quorn.

Here's Rossmore and Wicklow, from Erin's green shore,
Adair and Hill-Trevor, and one or two more,
Assembled together this fine hunting morn,
All eager to start and ride hard with the Quorn.

It boots not to tell all the deeds that were done
By the lords and the ladies that rode in the run,
How a fox broke away when the Coplow was drawn,
And fast at his heels came Tom Firr and the Quorn.

How we sped o'er the pasture, o'er hill and o'er dale,
By Billesdon, and Norton, and Skeffington Vale,
O'er oxer and timber, through brake, bush and thorn,
In the first thirty minutes we rode with the Quorn.

Tell me not of the sport that the Meath can afford,
Of the walls of Kildare, or the runs with the Ward;
Till the Leicestershire pastures grow turnips and corn,
Still, still let me linger and ride with the Quorn.

Then high fill the bowl, let the bumper go round;
Here's a health to the horse, here's a health to the hound;
Here's a health to the huntsman, a health to his horn,
A toast to ourselves, and three cheers for the Quorn.

APPENDIX

APPENDIX I

TOM FIRR'S HUNTING DIARY FOR 1883-84

It is appropriate that the first biography of Tom Firr is published a century after the season which was eulogised by Brooksby, the finest of correspondents, as The Best Season on Record. Brooksby wrote a book about it and in the forefront of those who took part in that memorable season was Tom Firr. By coincidence, Tom wrote in the final entry in the diary, "And so ended the best season I ever saw." For a hundred years hunting people have speculated about Tom's own versions of the tremendous runs that were enjoyed. They are published for the first time by kind permission of his granddaughter, Mrs. Grace Pickard.

1883

Commenced cubhunting on
Monday, Sept 17th at Quorn Woods. Found some cubs, but scent was bad. Ran one to ground. Then went on to the Brand. Soon got in among a litter and killed one.

Wednesday 19th

Stanford Park. Found cubs and killed one after a good deal of work then and at Normanton Hills.

Friday 21st

Costock for Bunny. Found a fair show of cubs. Ran one to ground and killed another in Wysall village after a good morning's work.

Monday 24th

Ashby Pastures. Found a splendid lot of cubs and after three hours of good work, during which time five brace at least went away, we killed one.

Thursday 27th

One Barrow Lodge. No cubs, only a brace of old foxes, found either here or Gisborne's Gorse, Charley, Cat Hill and Birch Hill.

Friday 28th

Barkby Holt. Found some cubs there and killed a brace. Went to Baggrave, John o'Gaunt and the Coplow, but little could be done on account of standing corn.

OCTOBER

Monday, October 1st

Gartree Hill. No cubs. Found a good lot in Thorpe Trussels and killed one from Cream Gorse.

Tuesday 2nd

Swithland. Found a good lot of cubs in Swithland and the Brand and killed one after plenty of work. Drew the Park coverts blank and came home.

Friday 5th

Widmerpool New Inn. Drew the Fish Pond Spinney blank. Went away with an old fox from Owthorpe Borders and ran to ground in Hoe Hill, South Notts covert, after a nice gallop. Came back (through) Roehoe, got on some cubs and killed one.

Monday 8th

Cossington Gorse. Found a small litter there and went on to Thrussington Wolds, when we got on an old fox and killed him in Ragdale Village after a short gallop. Shoby Scholes held a brace, one of which went to ground after a good dusting.

Tuesday 9th

Charley Crossroads. Bad day, only found one fox.

Friday 12th

Gaddesby. Capital morning. Killed a brace after good work, the second fox (an old one) having kept hounds going for two hours — both found in Mr. Cheney's spinneys.

Monday 15th

Six Hills. A nice gallop from Saxelby Old Wood to Lord Aylesford's covert and back to Shoby was all that was done.

Tuesday 16th

Woodhouse. First drew the osier bed at Tucker's brickyard blank, then went on to Burleigh and Hollywell Woods and the Privets. Found an old fox here, and with a capital scent. Hounds raced him through Longcliffe towards Shepshed, back the same line, then through Whittle Hill nearly to the Beacon, through the oak woods, away to Burleigh Hall, to Booth Wood, across Garendon Park and on to Hathern and nearly to Oakley

136

Wood; back again to Dishley, where he beat us after a really nice run, hounds beating horses out of sight.

Friday 19th

Barkby Hall. A wet morning, but a good day's sport was the result. Found first in a small spinney near the Holt and killed him after a short ring. Found next in Barkby Thorpe Spinney and lost him in the village. Went on to Scraptoft. Found in the long spinney. Ran nicely through the gardens and away by Keyham towards the Holt, but bore to the right by the Foxholes and on by Ingarsby to the Coplow. Changed foxes and gave it up.

Monday 22nd

Lodge on the Wolds. Found a ringing fox first in Owthorpe Borders. Afterwards got away with a good one from Kinoulton Gorse and had a very nice gallop indeed by Colston Bassett to Kaye Wood. Changed foxes and gave it up.

Tuesday 23rd

Oakley Wood. Found there and ran to Garendon and lost him. Scent bad. Found in the Outwoods and, with a better scent, twisted him about sharp for half an hour, when he crept into a small drain from which we could have pulled him out easily, but dare not do so through the scarcity of foxes.

Friday 26th

Ashby Pastures. Plenty of foxes but no scent in the morning. Afterwards finding in Mr. Cheney's spinney, hounds ran as if tied to their fox for thirty minutes, all over a good line, by Brooksby and Rearsby, back by Gaddesby, to ground under the road at Brooksby, a hundred yards only in front of them. This was a very fine gallop.

Saturday 27th

Sale of Cubhunters.

Monday 29th

Willoughby. Very foggy but a good day's sport. Found in the Gorse, ran to Widmerpool and back again, when scent altogether failed. Went on to Ella's Gorse, found, went away over the brook at a cracking pace to the Old Dalby, 25 minutes; then going towards Lord Aylesford's Covert and Thrussington Wolds, when it came on so foggy we could hardly see, and gave it up.

Tuesday 30th

Costock. A capital morning's sport. Found in Bunny New Wood and ran a cracker by Wysall to Willoughby Gorse to ground in the stick heap. Left him and went back to Bunny. Found in Rancliffe Wood and ran prettily by Bradmore, Ruddington, Edwalton and Tollerton, when he beat us.

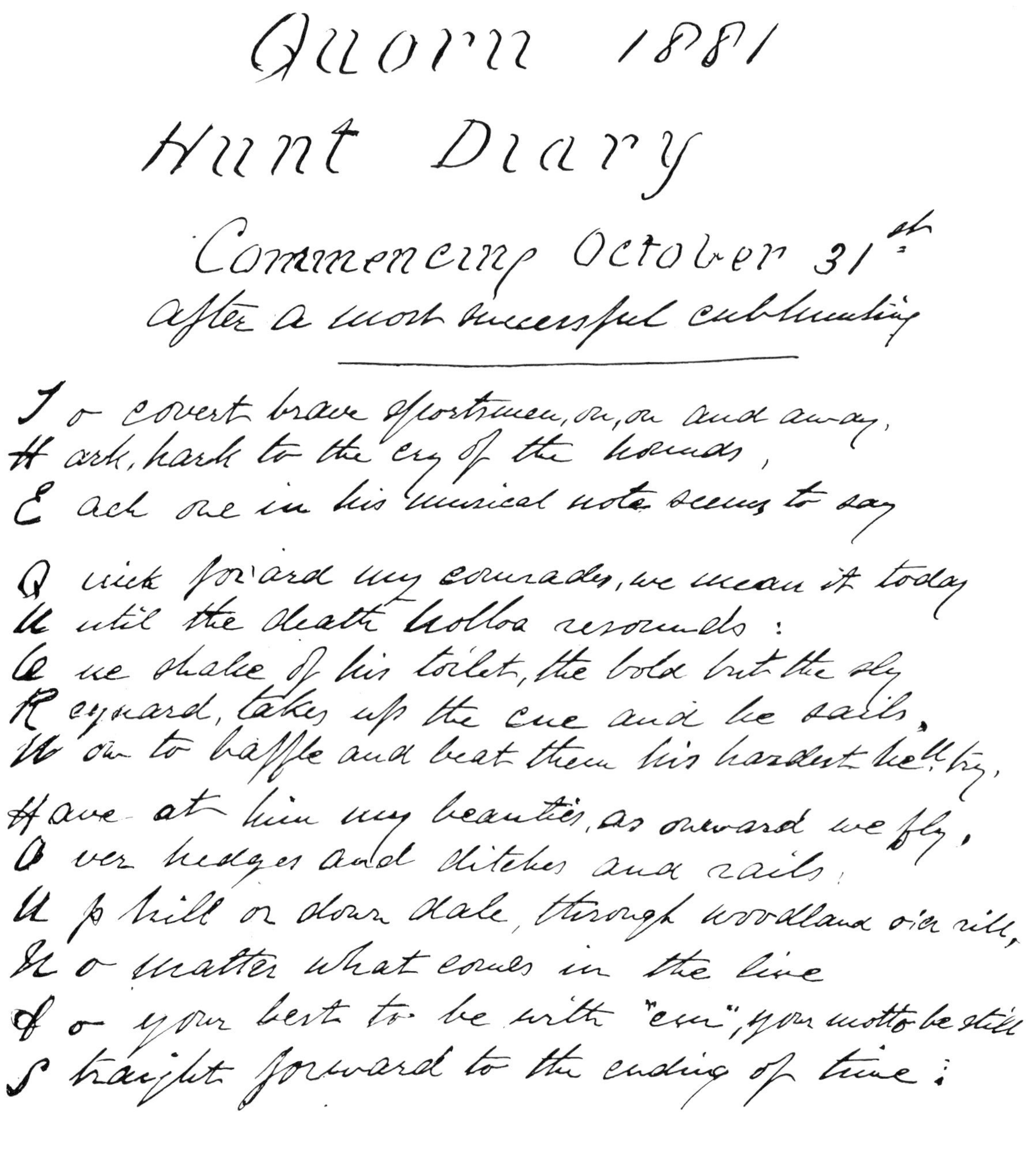

Quorn 1881

Hunt Diary

Commencing October 31st
after a most successful cubhunting

T o covert brave sportsmen, on, on and away,
H ark, hark to the cry of the hounds,
E ach one in his musical note seems to say

Q uick for'ard my comrades, we mean it today
U ntil the death hollow resounds :
O ut shake of his toilet, the bold but the sly
R eynard, takes up the cue and he sails,
N ow to baffle and beat them his hardest he'll try,
H ave at him my beauties, as onward we fly,
O ver hedges and ditches and rails
U p hill or down dale, through woodland o'er rill,
N o matter what comes in the line
D o your best to be with "em", your motto be still
S traight forward to the ending of time :

Figure 1.1 Specimen pages from Tom's *Hunting Diaries*

138

Cub hunting began later this
year than any I ever remember
and yet I think it was altogether
the most successful - The ground
being in capital order and
scent generally good. Cubs
plentiful in all parts of the
grass Country, while on the
Forest side I am sorry this
was not the case, for contrary
to the rule they were much fewer
here than in the open country

Friday, November 2nd

Round Hill, Syston. Found in the osier bed and killed there. Went on the Scraptoft, found and ran very prettily by Thurnby, towards Norton Gorse, then to the left back to Scraptoft, Keyham and Beeby, to ground in a drain between here and Barkby Holt.

NOVEMBER

Monday, November 5th

Regular hunting commenced at Kirby Gate. There was a good sized field out and a first class day's sport. Went as usual to Gartree Hill, found and away at once over the Burton flats, round towards Leesthorpe, by the Wheathills and into the shrubbery at Little Dalby; back by Wheathills and through Bury (Berry) Gorse, on by Whissendine, Ashwell, to Teigh House, where they rolled him over in the garden. Time an hour and twenty minutes. Drew Sir Francis's Covert blank. Found Thorpe Trussels and ran hard by Great Dalby, over Burrow (Burrough) Hill to Mr. Chaplin's home. Lost him there. Refreshed and came home.

Tuesday 6th

Bradgate Park. Drew several coverts blank. Found in Benscliffe, ran to ground on the Brand. Afterwards found in Quorn Wood, but had no sport.

Friday 9th

Lowesby Hall. Drew John o'Gaunt blank, but a fox got up in an adjoining turnip field, came into the covert and was killed. Larges' Spinney and Lord Morton's Gorse blank. Found in Botany Bay and ran to ground by Ingarsby. Went on to the Foxholes, found and had a very nice run, the fox getting to ground at last dead beat and just in front of them; the line being by Keyham and Beeby towards the Holt, turned towards Baggrave, then by Hungarton, to ground near Keyham. Bolted him and ran over nearly the same line again and back to the Foxholes to ground.

Saturday 10th

Hathern Turn. Not much sport. Found and killed in Oakley Wood, drew several coverts blank. Found in the Outwoods, a bad fox, and lost him on the Beacon.

Monday 12th

Wartnaby stone pits. No scent in the morning. Found in Holwell Mouth and marked him to ground in the stone pit spinney. Our next fox was found in Grimston Gorse, and although scent was bad at the commencement it improved and a very nice run was the result. Going away by Old Dalby Wood, then to the right through Saxelby Wood and on to Welby Fishponds; then round and by Cant's Thorns, back through Grimston and Dalby Wood, by Old Dalby Village and on to Lord Aylesford's Covert, away towards Grimston and he ran us out of scent between there and Shoby.

Tuesday 13th

Swithland. (Frosty morning). Found in Benscliffe Wood after drawing a lot of coverts blank and ran for a couple of hours, the line being by Ulverscroft, Markfield, towards Bardon, back to Benscliffe, by Newtown Linford and Ulverscroft again and back to Benscliffe, where we gave it up.

Friday 16th

Baggrave. First time of meeting here since poor General Burnaby's death. Found and killed one fox in covert. Went away with another and ran a cracker a ring towards Barkby Holt and Hungarton and back to the covert; swinging once round it, they went way to the right of the Hall, then to the left by the osier bed. Crossing the brook here, I pounded the whole field on bay mare, *My Darling*. Hounds kept racing away up to the top round, to the left of Thimble Hall and on to the left of Twyford. Then pretty straight to Thorpe Trussels, sharp to the left without touching the covert and on by Ashby Pastures, Cream Gorse, to ground just beyond. Capital 45 minutes. After leaving the drain, the fox bolted and we ran him to ground again beyond Guadaloupe. The day now changed much for the worse, thick fog and rain. Found in Thorpe Trussels and, after a hunting run, gave it up.

Saturday 17th

Prestwold. Drew the coverts blank. Then went to Bunny. Found at once in a drenching rain. Did no good. Came home with boots full of water.

Monday 19th

Ratcliffe-on-the Wreake. Very wild and stormy. We found in Cossington Gorse and also in Walton Thorns but hounds could not run. Found another fox in Lord Aylesford's Covert and killed him in Grimston Gorse.

Tuesday 20th

Narborough Crossroads. The usual crowd of footpeople here to head the fox, yet we had a remarkably pretty forty minutes. Found him in the Bogs and ran by Whetstone and Countesthorpe to Peatling, when he beat us, the earths all being open! Went back to Enderby, found, and killed him in fifteen minutes.

Friday 23rd

Rearsby. A splendid day's sport! Found our first fox in one of Mr. Cheney's spinneys and ran very prettily for thirty minutes, the line being by Gaddesby and Ashby, then to the right of Barsby and South Croxton, to ground under Queniborough spinney. Barkby Holt being our next draw, we found in the gorse and such a scent was there that hounds raced clean away from all but about a half dozen. Through Baggrave Covert, then by the Hall and Carbridge, leaving it just on the right; also Lowesby, then by Springfield Hill as if for John o'Gaunt. Turned to the right by Tilton Mill, afterwards passing that village and ran by Skeffington Wood, Tilton Wood, Robin-a-Tiptoe and Launde Wood. Foxes were unfortunately changed, so did not kill. The hunted fox was picked up, dead beat, on the line near Twyford viaduct, was put in a bag, carefully nursed, and turned down at Baggrave. Time of the run altogether about an hour, the first 30 minutes quite at racing pace. I was riding the bay mare, *My Darling*, who carried me splendidly.

Saturday 24th

Copt Oak. A nice day's sport. Found Hammercliffe Wood, ran by Blackhill, then to the left under the Beacon, by Charley Knoll, Ives Head, One Barrow, and he got to ground, in view, in the rocks near Grace Dieu. Found next in Gisborne's Gorse and finished there after a pretty ring of thirty minutes.

Monday 26th

Widmerpool New Inn. Found our first fox in Curate's Gorse and went away very quickly towards Upper Broughton, then turning to the left, ran over Hickling Standard, by that village, then along the vale by Sherbrooke's Covert and on to Nether Broughton, by the vicarage, then turning to the right ran back to Hickling Standard, over the top and killed him just below. Very pretty run. Found next in Roehoe, and ran hard by Kinoulton Gorse, just to the left of Owthorpe Borders, through Wynnstay Planting, round to the right of Cotgrave Gorse, straight away over the valley; swam the canal and killed him in the open beyond Stragglethorpe, on the way to Nottingham.

Tuesday 27th

Rothley House. Blank day. Drew Glenfield and coverts back, Mr. Paget's Gorse, Sir A. Palmer's coverts, Rothley coverts, Swithland Wood, Brand etc., etc.

Friday 30th

Great Dalby. After looking for an outlying fox we went on to Gartree Hill, found, and were away at once over the hill, by Great Dalby, thence by the old windmill and round by Thorpe Satchville; to the left by Adam's Gorse and over the Burrow steeplechase course, up to that village and then to Mr. Chaplin's home. The pace up to this had been capital, but now storms came and scent got bad. We afterwards hunted him by the Punch Bowl and Little Dalby and he beat us near Sir Francis Burdett's Covert. We then went on to Thorpe Trussels, found and went away by the village and straight to Burrow Hills. The fox here being headed, we came back by Sir Francis's covert, thence between Gartree Hill and Great Dalby, nearly to Kirby, and back to Ashby Pastures, where we stopped them, as it was late. Good day's sport.

DECEMBER

Saturday, December 1st

Cotes Toll Bar. Fair day's sport. Found a brace at Stanford and killed the second near Kingston Hall.

APPENDIXES

Monday 3rd

Six Hills. Another clinking good day. Went first to Ella's Gorse, found, and away over the brook at once, towards Willoughby, but when near it we turned to the right and ran over a lot of good country by Old Dalby and through Lord Aylesford's Covert to ground in Shoby Scholes. Time about forty minutes. Finding next in Thrussington Wolds, hounds ran a cracker and rolled him over in the open between Broughton and Long Clawson, after passing by Lord Aylesford's, Dalby Wood, Holwell Mouth, then into the vale. Time fifty minutes.

Tuesday 4th

Quorn House. Not much sport. Wild stormy day. Found in Quorn Wood and lost him at Swithland. Found next in Benscliffe and ran to ground at Ulverscroft. Afterwards found in Hammercliffe and on the Beacon, where we killed him.

Friday 7th Lowesby Hall and **Saturday 8th** Costock, frost — no hunting.

Monday 10th

Willoughby. Found in the Gorse. Went away by Ella's, thence to the left by Old Dalby, down nearly to Lord Aylesford's Covert, then to the left again by Dalby Wood, through Grimston Gorse and Saxelby Wood. Thence over the nice line of grass towards Welby. Turning to the left near Cant's Thorns, we ran on to, and straight through Old Hills and nearly to Melton spinney; to the left by Scalford Mill, Landyke Lane, and keeping Piper Hole and Clawson Thorns just on the right, ran him to ground in Holwell Mouth. Time an hour and fifty minutes. Fine hunting run. We afterwards found in Thrussington New Covert, but storms came on. Could not run.

Tuesday 11th

Charley Crossroads. Blank day. Drew Birch Hill, Bardon, Charley, Cat Hill, Gisborne's Gorse, all the One Barrow coverts, Iveshead, Outwoods, Mucklin Wood, etc.

Friday 14th

Thorpe Satchville Hall. A very miserable morning. Found in Thorpe Trussels, but as soon as we got away a terrible storm came on and at Dalby not an atom of scent was left. Back to Ashby Pastures, found and had a very nice gallop of forty minutes, first by the the Trussels, then to the right over the nice line of grass by Ashby Folville and Gaddesby, towards Queniborough Spinney. The fox being headed back downwind spoilt it altogether, for upwind they ran well, but in the other direction could not run at all. We afterwards found in Barkby Holt and ran the same line as on Friday 23rd November (but not so fast quite) to Tilton, the fox beating us in the village, where he was seen not two minutes in front of the hounds. This was a real nice gallop.

143

Saturday 15th

Lodge on the Wolds. Found first in Lord Manners's Coverts and lost him after a ring on the plough. Found again in the same coverts and ran for over three hours in the neighbourhood of Owthorpe, Kinoulton, Roehoe, thence by Kinoulton Gorse, Stonepit Spinney, Cotgrave Gorse and on to Hoe Hill, (at least up to the canal beside it), then back by the Lime Kilns to Colston Bassett, where this stout fox was rolled over in the open, the last hour and a quarter being at good pace. Horses all beat.

Monday 17th

Wartnaby Hall. A terribly cold day and all that was done was a nice gallop from Welby osier bed, by Old Hills and back again. Time thirty minutes.

Tuesday 18th

Again a long hunting run of over three hours. Met at Ulverscroft Hall and, after drawing several coverts blank, found in Hammercliffe and stopped the hounds at Swithland through darkness.

Friday 21st

Beeby. Found in Scraptoft and hunted with the worst scent seen this season, by Ingarsby, Quenby, Baggrave, to Barsby, when he was lost. Went back to Barkby Holt, found, and killed the fox who had given us the two good runs to Tilton and beyond. He was now quite mangy. We afterwards found in Mr. Cheney's triangle covert, and hounds getting away on his back fairly raced to Brooksby, turned back downwind when the pace was slow, and we gave it up near Rearsby.

Saturday 22nd

Costock. Another splendid day's sport. Found in Bunny Old Wood, ran through the Intake then by Wysall to Hoton, by Burton, Walton, through Mr. Cradock's ash spinney, by Six Hills, over Mr. Coupland's farm towards Old Dalby; thence at a much greater pace and over a beautiful line by Broughton Station, to the right of Curate's Gorse and on to Parson's Thorns, but not into it. On now towards Kinoulton Gorse, then to the right by Kinoulton and Hickling, to Kaye Wood. Keeping just to the right of this, we ran on now by Colston Bassett to Langar, where we were obliged to stop them for want to daylight. The run occupied considerably over three hours. There were parts of fast, parts slow and parts at fair hunting pace, the country crossed being nearly all grass and the distance 23 miles. It was most unfortunate not having more light, as the fox was dead beat and only a short distance in front. Hounds must soon have caught him, as they richly deserved. Only four or five saw the end.

Monday 24th

Six Hills. Found at Cossington Gorse and ran to ground below Thrussington. Found next in Thrussington New Covert and went at an awful pace by the ash spinney, towards Burton, which we afterwards passed after one or two turns. Then ran on to Prestwold, where we lost him, the last part not being nearly so fast as the first 15 minutes. Went back to Thrussington Wolds, found and ran to ground after a lively twelve minutes on Mr. Henton's farm at Hoby.

Friday 28th

Brooksby Hall. An outlying fox from a stubble field by the Rotherby Spinneys gave us a ringing run, being frequently headed, and was lost near Cream Gorse. Found next in Ashby Pastures and hounds ran very smartly by Thorpe Satchville, Great Dalby, Guadaloupe and nearly to Melton, when he beat us.

Monday 31st

Widmerpool New Inn. A very fine hunting run was brought off today. Found in Curate's Gorse, ran by the New Inn, thence to the left by Willoughby and round into the vale, by Upper Broughton and Sherbrooke's Covert. Then to the right by the other Broughton and Wartnaby Hills, Little Belvoir and Holwell Mouth. Back again into the valley by Clawson, a ring, and again over the Hills and on by Grimston Gorse and Lord Aylesford's Covert, by Ragdale and over the Hoby raspers, at one of which Count Kinsky got an awful fall which laid him out! Hounds in the meantime running on towards Cossington Gorse, thence by Seagrave and Pawdy, by Walton, towards Wymeswold and back to the right in a line for, and near to, Old Dalby, where hounds were stopped for want of daylight with the fox dead beat just in front of them. Out of a large field, seven only got to the end of this excellent run.

JANUARY 1884

Friday, January 4th

Keyham. Found at Scraptoft and, after a twisting run by Queniborough and Barkby Holt, cleverly hunted by hounds, he was killed at Gaddesby Spinneys. Found next in Ashby Pastures, but he was such a short-running fox, showed but very little sport.

Saturday 5th

Costock. Found in the twigs, Prestwold and ran to ground at Costock. Real pretty 20 minutes. Bolted him and ran by Stanford to Normanton village and back to the Dog Kennel Wood at Stanford, when darkness stopped further proceedings. Nice afternoon's sport.

Monday 7th

Old Dalby. Another splendid day's sport. Found in Grimston Gorse and ran at a tremendous pace through Saxelby Wood, by Wartnaby, to the left of Cant's Thorns and Welby and on by Old Hills and Wycomb to Goadby Gorse, to ground in the main earths not a hundred yards in front of hounds. A finer 45 minutes could not be seen. Found in Welby fishponds and ran fast for 20 minutes, then a good hunting pace by Melton spinney, towards Freeby Wood; back to the left by Wycomb and stopped hounds at dark at Melton spinney. Fine day's sport. Last run an hour and 20 minutes.

Friday 11th

Great Dalby. Found in Burrow Hill spinney and ran in a blustering wind, by the Punch Bowl and on to Pickwell, round to the left, back to Leesthorpe to ground. Our next fox was found in Thorpe Trussels and, with a wonderful improvement in the atmosphere, hounds ran a cracker, the line being through Adam's Gorse and over the steeplechase course, thence by Burdett's Covert, Gartree Hill, over the Burton flats by Berry Gorse, towards Brentingby, then to the left by the riverside to Burbage's Covert, straight through and away by Burton, towards Stapleford Park, rolling him over when within three fields of it. Splendid run. Time a little over an hour.

Saturday 12th

Hathern Turn. Another really good day. Finding in Garendon home covert, hounds hunted him beautifully by the Privets, Whittle Hill, the Beacon, thence away to Hammercliffe towards Bardon and round Groby, when the first check of any consequence occurred. Time 50 minutes. Recovering the line they ran through Bradgate Old Wood and other of their coverts and killed him at the end of two hours and a quarter, all capital hunting.

Monday 14th

Six Hills. After hunting a fox slowly from Cossington Gorse to Hoby, we went to Thrussington New Covert, found a very fine fox and ran him an hour and three minutes and bowled him over in the open; the line being by Six Hills, then towards Shoby Scholes, then to the left over the Six Hills road and on towards Wymeswold, but bearing to the right, passed Old Dalby, thence by Lord Aylesford's Covert and Shoby and round by Ragdale, killing him just beyond; the fox standing up stiff as a crutch when dead, without the slightest assistance. Walton Thorns gave us the next fox and him they ran at top speed for 15 minutes and knocked him over. Another being holloa'd for'ard at the same time, we raced him through Mr. Cradock's ash spinney, then towards Wymeswold, keeping on the left of Ella's Gorse. We soon passed Willoughby and Wysall and ran on to Widmerpool, when darkness beat us. Grand day's sport.

Tuesday 15th

Charley Crossroads. Found at One Barrow and raced away to Blackbrook. Hounds divided, the body racing away to Grace Dieu to ground, the others killing their fox in a pig sty near the White Horse. We afterwards found on the Whitwick Rocks and ran him hard for forty minutes by Holly Hayes, Bawdon Hill, Gisborne's Gorse and Charley, and killed him at Green Hill Farm.

Thursday 17th

Prestwold at 12. The day after Loughborough Ball. A beautiful morning for a meet of the kind and one or two charming runs followed. Willoughby Gorse provided the first fox, when hounds raced away to Widmerpool and rolled him over in fifteen minutes. Curate's Gorse gave us our next, and such a 32 minutes he gave us that is not often seen. Going

APPENDIXES

away the usual line over the Broughton Road, then towards Hickling Standard, round to the right by the Broughtons and Sherbrooke's Covert, towards Kaye Wood and round to Hickling, where they rolled him over handsomely in the open.

Friday 18th

Quenby Hall. A fox was first disturbed on the park by the foot people, who went to ground below Ingarsby. Botany Bay gave us the next, a beautifully fine fox who went away at once by Tomlin's Spinney, Billesdon windmill, Skeffington, Rolleston, Keythorpe, East Norton, and rolled him over in the open near Loddington. A very fine run. Time something over an hour. Afterwards found in John o'Gaunt and ran to ground at Tilton Station.

Monday 21st

Asfordby. Finding a fox in Welby osier bed, we went away at pace for a long journey over the Belvoir country, frequently changing foxes on the way. We ran first by Kettleby, then by Old Hills, Melton Spinney, Wycomb, nearly to Freeby Wood. Passed Goadby Gorse, then to Harby Hills, Eastwell, nearly to Belvoir Castle and back to Croxton Park when, being on another fresh fox and scent bad, it was given up.

Tuesday 22nd

Woodhouse Eaves. Found first at Blackbird's Nest and killed him below the Outwoods. Found next in the Privets and ran to ground at Shepshed after a pretty gallop. Bolted him, and ran to ground again at Burleigh Wood, and left him.

Friday 25th

Ashby Folville. Found in Thorpe Trussels and lost him after a hunting run by Burdett's Covert, Punch Bowl, Pickwell and Cold Overton. Found next in Ashby Pastures and, after as fine a run as could possibly be seen, killed him handsomely at Stapleford Park; the line being first towards Gaddesby, then along the Ashby Valley, by Thorpe Trussels, then beneath Ashby Pastures towards Kirby, round to the right by Guadaloupe and Burton Lazars and into Burbage's Covert. As hounds entered we saw the fox going out at the other side, towards Brentingby, but, turning, he came back over the river and then crossed the Burton Flats, never being more than a field or a couple in front until they raced up to him and knocked him over. Time an hour and five minutes. We all came home from Melton by train.

Saturday 26th

Lodge on the Wolds. Found in Owthorpe Borders and ran very prettily for about 40 minutes. A ring it was, and at the end we nearly clashed with the Belvoir, who had brought a fox from Sherbrooke's Covert.

Monday 28th

Rearsby. Very frosty morning and we did not move off till 12 o'clock. No scent and very

147

little sport. We ran a fox to ground from Cossington Gorse; another from Walton Thorns, and a short ring from Lord Aylesford's Covert finished it.

Tuesday 29th

Charley Crossroads. A nice run over the forest from One Barrow, the first 15 minutes at a great pace. The fox was eventually lost near Bawdon Castle. Found afterwards in Longcliffe and ran to ground in Burleigh Wood.

FEBRUARY

Friday, February 1st

Queniborough. Another famous day's sport. Did not find until we got to John o'Gaunt. We then ran at tremendous pace over the wild open country towards Owston, then to the left by Somerby and Pickwell and on to Whissendine to ground. Time of this rattling good gallop, fifty minutes. Did not find again.

Saturday 2nd

Costock. Found at once in Bunny New Wood and ran very prettily by Costock, where the water was out, but the fox struggled through. Then running towards Leake and up by Stanford and Prestwold, when the hare-stained ploughs did away with scent, so that hounds could not much more than walk after him, after which we worked round towards Normanton and lost him. The Hoton brook was jumped by a few of us under Stanford Park, which caused some fun and excitement, as it is very wide. One only out of the seven cleared it, but only three of us fell.

Monday 4th

Widmerpool New Inn. Drew Curate's blank and went on to Willoughby. Found in the Gorse and ran to ground at once. After drawing Ella's and Walton Thorns blank we went on to Lord Aylesford's Covert, found and went away a cracker, leaving Grimston village on the left, then working round, ran through the Gorse and Saxelby Wood, by Old Dalby Wood and over the open to the station to ground beside the line. Charming 20 minutes. Having got a terrier, we quickly bolted the fox and ran him a capital ring by Dalby Wood, towards Six Hills and back to the drain at Dalby Station, the fox just saving himself and was left, although he might have been got out and eaten in a few minutes. The last run being as fast as the first made it a real good afternoon's sport.

Tuesday 5th

Rothley House. Drew several coverts blank. Found eventually on Swithland Wood and ran to ground below Maplewell.

Friday 8th

Quenby Hall at 12. Day after the Harboro' Ball, and there was a great field out, but the day's sport, although not a bad one, was not quite up to the average in this good season.

Finding first in Botany Bay, we ran rather prettily away on the Norton side and round by Old Frisby to Skeffington and lost him. Afterwards finding in Hungarton Foxholes, we ran by Baggrave to ground before reaching the Holt.

Saturday 9th

Dishley. Found in Piper Wood a vixen, and left her. Did not find again.

Monday 11th

Thrussington. A wild morning, still a capital day's sport was brought off. We first found in Cossington Gorse and hunted prettily down to Ratcliffe and Syston and back to Ratcliffe, to ground beside the Wreake. A tremendous storm coming on at the end wetted us through in five minutes. Found next in better weather in Thrussington Wolds. Hounds hunted their fox beautifully by Ragdale, Shoby and Hoby, thence by Grimston and Old Dalby towards the station. Then back and over Wartnaby Hills, through Saxelby Wood, the pace here increasing considerably. They were working up to their fox and racing away over the beautiful grasses. They ran through Saxelby village and on to Asfordby, when they bowled their fox over handsomely. Capital run.

Thursday 14th

Lord Lonsdale brought his hounds to Scraptoft by invitation. The day was pleasant in every respect and there was a great crowd. They found a fox in a small spinney below the farm and ran him to ground below Ingarsby. Finding next in the Bay, they went away at a good pace over the hills by Tomlin's Spinney and on by Tilton and Launde Woods, where they clashed with Sir Bache Cunard's hounds and ended the day.

Friday 15th

Gaddesby. Bitterly cold and scent bad. Found a vixen in Cream Gorse and left her. Ashby Pastures being blank, we went on to Thorpe Trussels, found and ran to ground beyond the village. Bolted the fox and then ran a ring, which occupied an hour and got back to Thorpe, the fox again going to ground beside the line. We bolted him again and ran into him in about 15 minutes. We afterwards found in Mr. Cheney's Spinney and ran fast to Brooksby and back.

Saturday 16th

Lodge on the Wolds. Awfully cold, scent bad, and no sport.

Monday 18th

Wartnaby Stone Pits. Another clinking day's sport. Found first, or at least had one found for us that had been got out of a drain that morning and down near Mr. Marsh's house. Hounds getting too close to him, they raced him to death in 12 minutes. Very pretty while it lasted. Finding next in Welby Fish Ponds, commenced as fine a run as ever was seen, as pace and country was so good. The line was by Cant's Thorns, Wartnaby Fish Ponds, Saxelby village, thence by Lord Aylesford's Covert and on to Ragdale, back to the left by

149

Shoby and Asfordby and back to our starting point. Fast 50 minutes. Quite first class. Passing the Fish Pond, we now ran on by Welby Church, thence to Old Hills, which was full of foxes, and notwithstanding that our fox was dead beat and just in front of us we changed here and got beat ourselves. Hounds richly deserved to have had him.

Thursday 21st

The first point-to-point steeplechase came off at Gaddesby, when 14 started, all farmers, and rode a line by Thorpe Satchville, then up to the Trussels and back to Mr. Cheney's park, Mr. J. Cash taking both the 14 and 12 stone races.

Friday 22nd

Baggrave Hall. The covert and others in a line to John o'Gaunt were blank. At the last named, a fox was found who gave us a tremendous spin for 15 minutes. Hounds almost flew and ran their fox to ground near Somerby. Billesdon Coplow produced the next and he too showed a capital run. Hounds raced away over the hills by Tilton, through its wood beyond and the chain of Cottesmore woods, by Launde and Withcote, when they lost their fox. I got a bad fall near Tilton Wood and could go on no farther, being brought home in Mr. Halston's dogcart.

Saturday 23rd

Wymeswold. They found at Bunny and were ringing about there all day.

Monday 25th

Six Hills. They found in Thrussington Wolds and lost their fox somewhere near Shoby Scholes. Finding next in Grimston Gorse, they hunted slowly for a time, when he beat them.

Friday 29th

Great Dalby. This being my first time out since my fall, I received many congratulations on being out again so soon. We had again a capital day's sport. Found first in Gartree Hill and ran for an hour and five minutes and killed him handsomely in the open. Among others out today was Luke, the jockey. The line we ran was over the Burton Flats, round to the right by the Punch Bowl, thence towards Owston Wood, but turning more to the right, we crossed over by Adam's Gorse and on to Guadaloupe and bowled him over near Sandy Lane. From Thorpe Trussels we had another nice gallop and killed the fox beside the brook at Ashby Folville. Drew Gaddesby Spinneys, then home.

MARCH

Saturday March 1st

Dishley. A very nice hunting run over the forest from the reed bed at Garendon, crossing the park, thence through Booth Wood and the Privets, by The Oaks Church to Gisborne's Gorse and to ground after more ringing about.

Monday 3rd

Kettleby. Wretched morning, the coldest rain I think I ever was out in, which continued more or less all day! No sport.

Friday 7th

Beeby. Large field out and among them Col. Anstruther Thomson. A nice day's sport, but nothing more. Finding first at Scraptoft we ran a ring in scorching sun and lost her, for it was no doubt a vixen. Found next in the Foxholes and ran to ground after a pretty gallop, and the same with our next fox from Queniborough Spinney.

Monday 10th

Widmerpool New Inn. Another first class day's sport. Found in Curate's Gorse and raced away towards Broughton, thence to Sherbrooke's Covert, covering this distance in 11 minutes. We then continued on over the vale by Hose Brickyard and round by Clawson, through Clawson Thorns to Piper Hole Gorse. Time up to here forty-five minutes. Hounds here divided and, with horses all too beat to get near them, one lot went on and ran their fox to ground at Harby Hills. The others ran over a great deal more country and ran their fox to ground at Old Hills.

Tuesday 11th

Kirby Muxloe. Although foxes are very scarce in this neighbourhood, we found one in Narborough Bogs today and had a very nice run with him by Whetstone and Countesthorpe to Peatling Gorse to ground.

Friday 14th

Barkby Hall. Found first a vixen in Botany Bay and stopped hounds. John o'Gaunt supplied us with another, but he did not show us much sport. Late in the afternoon we had a pretty run from Thorpe Trussels, going first towards the Pastures, but turning sharp to the left by Adam's Gorse and over Burrow Hills to the Punch Bowl. Straight through towards Cold Overton, then to the left by Leesthorpe and Bury Gorse, to some other spinneys which were wanted for the Cottesmore the next day, so I had orders to stop the hounds, and when their fox was dead beat and just in front of them.

Saturday 15th

Lodge on the Wolds. A nice day's sport. Hounds ran fast with a fox from Wynnstay Gorse, 15 minutes to ground; and afterwards finding in Lord Manver's coverts and Owthorpe Borders made up a hard day by ringing about on the ploughs.

Monday 17th

Six Hills. No sport. Not a fox could be found but vixens, and then of course we did not run. There was one in Thrussington Wolds and another in Cossington Gorse.

Tuesday 18th

Copt Oak. A fox was found in Dr. Wright's coverts and another in the Brook Spinney, near Thurcaston Gorse. Not much sport.

Friday 21st

Great Dalby. Found in Gartree Hill and ran very prettily over Burrow Hill, through the Punch Bowl and on to Cold Overton. Up to this it was all nice going and at a fair pace, but afterwards, turning to the left, we got on dry fallows and it was nothing but slow hunting, the line being through Ranksborough, thence by Teigh and Ashwell, and we gave it up just beyond. We then trotted by to Thorpe Trussels, found, and stopped the hounds after running through the Punch Bowl and in a line for Leesthorpe.

Saturday 22nd

Charley Crossroads. A fox was found and almost immediately killed on the Whitwick Rocks. Another, from the reservoir, gave us a really fine hunting run of over two hours, when he laid down on some fallows near the Beacon and hounds picked him up, he being unable to stir. The line we ran was by One Barrow, Sharpley Rocks, round through the reservoir and on to Whitehorse Wood, by Shepshed, towards Piper, but keeping to the left ran on to Belton, then to the left to Grace Dieu. Over Sharpley Rocks, by One Barrow and over Ives Head. Thence by the end of Longcliffe to the Outwoods, and out against the Loughboro' Reservoir, when a long check occurred. Having got his line, we ran him back through the wood and away over Eason's Piece, by Whittle Hill and up to the Beacon Planting, at the lower end of which they rolled him over.

Monday 24th

Willoughby. We found in the Gorse and had a very pretty forty minutes, a ring, and lost the fox near Wysall. Afterwards finding a vixen in Curate's Gorse, she quickly went to ground. And another vixen was found in Mr. Cradock's ash spinney, which we did not run.

Friday 28th

Lowesby Hall. We first found an outlying one near Lowesby and raced him along by Carbridge to Halstead, back again to Lowesby, and keeping to the left of John o'Gaunt they rattled him along over the Twyford brook, by Marefield, to ground in a turf drain when pointing for Owston. Capital 25 minutes. A terrier being handy, we soon bolted him and rolled him over in another ten minutes. Botany Bay gave us a fox and a very nice gallop. Hounds fairly raced by Ingarsby to Scraptoft. Here I think we changed foxes, for scent was never so good after. Still, they hunted very prettily over the Uppingham road and on nearly to Norton Gorse, where we lost him.

APRIL

Tuesday April 1st

Brooksby at 1(pm). Cream Gorse held a vixen. Ashby Pastures was blank, but a good fox was found in Thorpe Trussels, who went away over the railway, and with a fair scent hounds ran very smartly by Great Dalby and Burdett's Covert, through Gartree Hill towards Burton, then by Capt. Ashton's house and Sandy Lane to Old Guadaloupe to ground. Time 45 minutes.

Monday 7th

Widmerpool New Inn. Curate's was blank, but we found in Parson's Thorns and had a pretty hunting run by the Broughtons to Little Belvoir, where they got up to their fox and fairly raced as far as Clawson Thorns, when he got to ground just in front of them.

Saturday 12th

Lodge on the Wolds. Last day. After drawing some time, we found in Wynnstay Planting and ran hard for 20 minutes, round by Roehoe, nearly to Kinoulton and back to Owthorpe Borders, when we got on the hard ploughs and nothing but slow hunting with a ringing fox was done.

And so ended the best season I ever saw.

Scarcity of foxes on the forest has caused one to leave out a few days on that side when really nothing could be done. Three brace of bad foxes killed which are not mentioned above.

APPENDIX II

THE TOM FIRR TESTIMONIAL FUND SUBSCRIBERS

The Tom Firr Testimonial Fund created unprecedented interest. No huntsman up to his time had been given anything like the sum which he received. Those who contributed formed a cross-section of society, headed by the Prince of Wales, and many of the families represented are still active in hunting today.

Receipts to the Fund totalled £3,468. Tom Firr was given a cheque for £3,200. Other payments included £32 for an inscribed presentation plate and £4 for a book containing the subscribers' names:

SUBSCRIBERS

	£	s.	d.			£	s.	d.
Ashton, Major	25	0	0	Barry, Capt. J. D.	5	5	0
Adderley, Alfred	10	10	0	Buckby, R. H.	5	5	0
Arkwright, J. T.	10	10	0	Birkin, R. S.	5	5	0
Allan, R. G.	10	0	0	Bouverie,			
Atkinson, Major	10	0	0	Major The Hon G.	5	0	0
Asquith, Mrs.	5	0	0	Brocklehurst, Mrs.	5	0	0
Allen, Van. J.	5	0	0	Biddulph, R. N.	5	0	0
Angus, Maxwell	2	2	0	Bentley, H. C.	5	0	0
Aldridge, C. H.	2	2	0	Barry, Capt. Lionel E.	5	0	0
Armstrong, A. E.	1	1	0	Blair, Col. F.	5	0	0
Aspinall, Miss	1	1	0	Bentinck, Lord Chas	5	0	0
Abbott, Capt. W. D.	1	0	0	Briggs, W.	3	3	0
				Bowmar, Walter	2	2	0
Barclay, H. T.	100	0	0	Bristowe, R. F.	2	2	0
Boden, H.	50	0	0	Beeby, Thos.	2	2	0
Baldock, E. H.	50	0	0	Burgess, Joseph	2	2	0
Belper, Lord	25	0	0	Bostock, Joseph	2	2	0
Brooks, Thos.	20	0	0	Braund, G. P.	2	2	0
Behrens, Frank	20	0	0	Boden, Walter	2	2	0
Bentinck,				Baillie, Col. J.	2	0	0
Lord William	15	0	0	Brooks, T. E.	2	0	0
Brocklehurst, Alfred	15	0	0	Burnaby, Miss	2	0	0
Boyce, Capt. T.	15	0	0	Bailey, A. C.	1	1	0
Brocklehurst, Col. J.	10	0	0	Bell, Miss N. J.	1	1	0
Burdett, Sir Francis	10	0	0	Brewitt, G. W.	1	1	0
Bourke,				Bryan, N.	1	1	0
Honble Harry	10	0	0	Black, H.	1	1	0
Bentinck,				Bouverie,			
Lord Henry	10	0	0	The Honble. S. P.	1	1	0
Baird, W.	10	0	0	Burrows, T. J.	1	1	0

Name	£	s	d
Bonser, E.	0	10	6
Cassell, Sir Ernest	100	0	0
Coats, G.	50	0	0
Coats, A.	50	0	0
Crawshaw, Lord	50	0	0
Cook, E. E.	25	0	0
Cradock, J. D.	25	0	0
Coventry, Arthur	25	0	0
Chaplin, Mr. and Mrs. Cecil	20	0	0
Chippindall, General	10	10	0
Chaplin, C. W.	10	0	0
Curzon, Lady Georgina	10	0	0
Cholmondeley, Col. H. C.	10	0	0
Charrington, H.	5	5	0
Corbett, Sir Walter	5	5	0
Curzon, Col. The Hon. M.	5	5	0
Chaplin, W. E.	5	5	0
Clarke, G. H.	5	5	0
Charrington, F.	5	0	0
Candy, Major	5	0	0
Candy, The Honble. Mrs.	5	0	0
Campbell, Mrs. Montgomery	5	0	0
Clarke, A. H.	5	0	0
Clarke, C. H.	5	0	0
Clark, J. W.	5	0	0
Cholmondeley, Lord	5	0	0
Clayton, E. C.	5	0	0
Churchill, Lord	5	0	0
Chaplin, The Right Hon. H.	5	0	0
Crossley, Sir Savile	5	0	0
Cannon, M.	5	0	0
Coleman, J. W.	3	3	0
Clifford, R. S., junr.	2	2	0
Cartmell, J. F.	2	2	0
Coxe, P. H.	2	2	0
Chaplin, Miss W.	2	2	0
Curnard, Gordon	2	0	0
Curzon, The Hon. Mrs. M.	1	1	0
Cradock, Thos.	1	1	0
Custance, H.	1	1	0
Chaplin, Miss B. M.	1	1	0
Close, James B.	1	0	0
Duncan, A. L.	50	0	0
De Winton, Walter	25	0	0
Durlacher, F. H.	20	0	0
Donisthorpe, Miss F.	10	10	0
De Lisle, Everard	10	0	0
Dudley, Lord	10	0	0
Dick, Quintin	5	0	0
Drummond, Capt.	3	3	0
De Lisle, Gerard	3	0	0
De Lisle, Edwin	2	2	0
Douglass, J. H.	1	1	0
Dashwood, Rev. C. D.	1	1	0
Dawkins, Mrs.	1	0	0
Ewing, Capt. J. R.	10	0	0
Essex, Earl of	10	0	0
Elmhirst, Capt. E. P.	3	3	0
Eaton, G. S.	3	3	0
Egerton, C. A.	2	2	0
Earp, G. H.	2	2	0
Ellis, Owen A.	2	2	0
Eaton, W. S.	1	1	0
Ewer, Amos	1	1	0
Ellis, Miss A. N.	1	1	0
Farquhar, Granville	25	0	0
Farquhar, Mrs.	10	0	0
Firth, Mrs. Mark	10	0	0
Fernie, C. W. B.	10	0	0
Forbes, J. F.	10	0	0
Fenwick, R. L.	10	0	0
Farley, Capt. Turner	10	0	0
Firth, Mark	10	0	0
Follett, Col.	5	5	0
Fletcher, H.	5	5	0
Fenwick, Noel	5	5	0
Fort, Richard	5	0	0
Farnham, G. F.	5	0	0
Falkner, R. A.	5	0	0
Fenwick, Guy	5	0	0
Fraser, Capt. H. Keith	5	0	0
Flude, Harry	3	3	0
Foster, W. H.	2	2	0
Forster, R.	2	2	0
Faire, J. E.	2	2	0
Freer, W. J.	1	1	0
Fitzherbert, Sir R.	1	1	0
Fox, J. H.	1	1	0
Foord-Kelcey, Rev. E.	0	10	6
Frank, L. W.	0	10	6
Gerard, Lady	25	0	0
Grenfell, Cecil	15	0	0
Greenall, Sir Gilbert	10	10	0
Grenfell, Mrs. Harry	10	0	0
Gibbs, A. W.	5	0	0
Gage, Col.	2	2	0
Gibbs, A. R.	1	1	0
Gilliat, H.	1	1	0
Gee, George	1	1	0
Gee, John	1	1	0
Guest, T. N.	1	0	0
Guest, Lady Theodora	1	0	0
Gillon, A.	1	0	0
Goodwill, —	1	0	0
Hartopp-Burns, Capt.	25	0	0
Henry, Col. T. A.	20	0	0
Hubbersty, W. P.	20	0	0
Herrick, Mrs. Perry	10	0	0
Hodson, George	10	0	0
Harrington, The Earl of	10	0	0
Hamilton, Honble. Gavin	10	0	0
Harriman, J.	5	5	0
Hillyard, Mrs.	5	5	0
Heygate, Capt. W. B.	5	0	0
Harrison, Capt. T. E.	5	0	0
Harter, J. F. Hatfield	5	0	0

	£	s.	d.
Hopetoun, The Earl of	5	0	0
Hardy, Gerald	5	0	0
Hope, Herbert	5	0	0
Hames & Son	5	0	0
Hanbury, Evan	5	0	0
Hartopp, Lady	5	0	0
Hanson, G. S.	5	0	0
Holden, Edward	5	0	0
Hibbert, C.	5	0	0
Hamshaw, H. A.	3	3	0
Hincks, H. T.	3	3	0
Hames, T. A.	3	3	0
Humphreys, J. H.	2	2	0
Hames, Miss	2	2	0
Hayward, J. A.	2	2	0
Humphreys, H.	2	2	0
Holden, John	2	0	0
Heymann, Albert	2	0	0
Hassall, Rev. G.	1	1	0
Harford, W. H.	1	1	0
Horsey, John	1	1	0
Hadden, Harvey	1	1	0
Hope, Edward	1	0	0
Holford, T.	1	0	0
Heseldyne, Godfrey	1	0	0
Isaacs, C.	0	10	0
Johnstone, Sir Frederick	25	0	0
Johnson, T. Fielding, junr.	3	3	0
James, H.	2	2	0
Knowles, R. M.	25	0	0
Knowles, A. M.	15	0	0
Kinsky, Count	10	0	0
Kenyon, Lord	5	0	0
Kavanagh, Capt. C.	3	0	0
Laycock, J. F.	100	0	0
Lubbock, B. W.	50	0	0
Lucas, A. C.	25	0	0
Lawson, Capt. W.	25	0	0
Lanesborough, Earl of	25	0	0
Lowther, Honble. L.	20	0	0
Lawson, H. L.	5	5	0
Lowther, Harold	5	5	0
Levy, M.	5	5	0
Lambton, Capt. The Hon. W.	5	0	0
Lonsdale, Dowager Countess	5	0	0
Loates, T.	5	0	0
Lever, A. Levy	3	3	0
Lockwood, B. W.	2	2	0
Lant, R.	2	2	0
Learoyd, Major, C. D.	1	1	0
Lant, J.	1	1	0
Lillingston, Capt. W. G.	1	1	0
Long, The Rt Hon. Walter	1	0	0
Logan, Col.	1	0	0
Monro, Russell	25	0	0
Muir, R. B.	20	0	0
Manners, Lord	20	0	0
Marlborough, The Duke of	20	0	0
Morgan, E. D.	10	0	0
Martin, W. J.	10	0	0
Murdock, Col. Burn	10	0	0
Markham, A. B.	10	0	0
Muir, Miss	7	7	0
McNeill, Mr. & Lady Hilda	5	5	0
Marshall, W. G.	5	0	0
Martin, R. F.	5	0	0
Mildmay, F. B.	5	0	0
Molyneux, Capt. The Hon. H.	5	0	0
Molyneux, The Hon. Mrs.	5	0	0
Martin, Arthur	5	0	0
Miles, W. F.	5	0	0
Morton, Lord	5	0	0
Marsh, R.	5	0	0
Moseley, Col. Paget	3	3	0
Manners, Lord Edward	3	0	0
Mayo, Thomas	2	2	0
Matthews, Mrs. George	1	1	0
Marriott, C. H.	1	1	0
Mackenzie, Austin	1	1	0
Musters, Mrs.	1	1	0
Martin, Rev. J.	1	1	0
Martin, Charles H.	1	0	0
Newcastle, The Duchess of	25	0	0
Newton, C. S.	5	0	0
Newton, Frank	5	0	0
Nuttall, T.	3	3	0
Nuttall, Dr. C. R.	2	2	0
Newark, Lord	1	0	0
O'Neal, Capt. Carter	10	10	0
Owen, Hugh	10	0	0
O'Shaughnessey, Col.	3	0	0
Osborne, J.	1	0	0
Portland, The Duke of	100	0	0
Paget, W. B.	100	0	0
Praed, H. B.	50	0	0
Paget, F. Walter	25	0	0
Paynter, Major	25	0	0
Paget, Sir Ernest	20	0	0
Packe, Hussey	10	0	0
Pennington, The Hon. Allan	10	0	0
Peake, W. A.	10	0	0
Parker, G. B.	10	0	0
Paget, J. Otho	10	0	0
Paulet, Lord and Lady Henry	5	5	0
Parker, Miss	5	0	0
Palmer, Sir Archdale	5	0	0
Paget, Mrs. W. B.	5	0	0
Pochin, W. A.	5	0	0
Phillips, C. J.	5	0	0

	£	s	d
Peterborough,			
The Bishop of	5	0	0
Peake, Frederick	5	0	0
Parker, C. T.	3	3	0
Paget, H. B.	2	2	0
Powell, Col. L. C.	2	2	0
Place, J. R.	2	2	0
Pettifor and Son	2	2	0
Podmore, E. B.	2	2	0
Portman,			
Hon. E. W. B.	2	0	0
Paget, Miss G.	2	0	0
Pochin, Capt. R.	1	1	0
Platt, J. E.	1	1	0
Paget, Miss H.	1	1	0
Paget, Miss Hylda	1	1	0
Parr, J. G.	1	1	0
Payne, W.	1	1	0
Prodgers, Rev. C.	1	1	0
Palmer, E. G. B.	1	0	0
Paget, W. E.	1	0	0
Paget, Miss M.	1	0	0
Ritchie, Thomas	10	10	0
Ratcliff, R. H.	10	0	0
Rolleston, Sir John	10	0	0
Robinson, H. Abbot	5	5	0
Rutland, The Duke of	5	0	0
Riddel, Capt.			
& Lady Evelyn	5	0	0
Robinson, John	5	0	0
Rolleston, L.	5	0	0
Roden, W. T.	2	2	0
Rawnsley, P.	2	0	0
Redfern, H.	1	1	0
Rolleston, S.	1	1	0
Ritchie, R.	1	0	0
Ritchie, A.	1	0	0
Scott, Sir Samuel	50	0	0
St. Maur, Lord Percy	25	0	0
St. Maur,			
Lord Ernest	25	0	0
Somerset,			
The Duke of	25	0	0
Stirling, Major G.	10	0	0
Smith, Capt. A. G.	10	0	0
Smith, G. Murray	10	0	0
Schwabe, A. J.	5	0	0
Smith, R. W.	5	0	0
Salvin, H.	5	0	0
Shakespear, C. B.	5	0	0
Story, H. V.	5	0	0
Sheriffe, R.	5	0	0
Smith, F. A.	5	0	0
Sargeant, J. F.	3	3	0
Swan, R. C.	2	2	0
Smith, W. K.	2	2	0
Smith, Henry	2	2	0
Stanley, Mrs. Sloane	2	2	0
Sheriffs, Rev. F. M.	2	0	0
Stafford, C. H.	1	1	0
Story, Miss	1	1	0
Story, Charles	1	1	0
Sutherland,			
The Duchess of	1	1	0
Sherbrooke, Capt. W.	1	1	0
Shaw, J. junr.	1	1	0
Smith, Charles	0	10	6
Trew, J. P.	25	0	0
Tennant, Major	20	0	0
Tennant,			
The Honble. Mrs.	10	0	0
Tuyll, Baron Max De	10	0	0
Trevor, Lord	10	0	0
Tidmas, J. B.	5	0	0
Thomson,			
Col. Anstruther	5	0	0
Tailby, W. W.	5	0	0
Turner, A.	5	0	0
Tempest,			
Lord Henry Vane	5	0	0
Tollemache,			
Hon. L. P.	5	0	0
Thomson, Stuart	5	0	0
Taylor, John	3	3	0
Taylor, H. Clough	3	3	0
Thompson, Sir H. W.	2	2	0
Taylor, J. W.	2	2	0
Turton, R. B.	2	2	0
Tyler, Thomas	2	2	0
Turner, Thomas, junr.	1	1	0
Thurlow, James	1	1	0
Tomkinson, J.	1	0	0
Thursby, Mrs.	0	10	0
Unitt, Dr. J.	5	5	0
Vaughan, R. N.	1	1	0
Warner, Capt. W. P.	50	0	0
Wilton, The Countess of			
and Mr. Pryor	50	0	0
Warner, E. H.	25	0	0
Wilson,			
Capt. Gordon	25	0	0
Wilson, Clarence	25	0	0
Winterbottom, W. D.	20	0	0
Wilson, H. H.	20	0	0
Wilson, George	10	10	0
Wright, William	10	0	0
Wilson, B.	10	0	0
Wood, Gordon	10	0	0
Woodward, Mr.			
and Mrs. Hawkes	5	5	0
Welch, H. R.	5	5	0
Worswick, Col. R. W.	5	5	0
Warwick,			
The Countess of	5	0	0
Wade, G. T.	5	0	0
Wales, His Royal Highness			
The Prince of	5	0	0
Wright, C. W.	5	0	0
Wroughton, W.	5	0	0
Willett, Capt. Saltren	5	0	0
Wolverton, Lord	5	0	0
Williamson, G.	5	0	0
Wade, Miss	3	3	0
Wickham, H.	3	3	0
Walding, S. W.	3	3	0
Wood, Major D. E.	2	2	0
Wright, Frank	2	2	0
Wells, E. E.	2	2	0

Wells, S. B.	...	...	...	2	2	0			
Whetstone, W. F.		...		2	0	0			
Worcester,									
The Marquis of		...		2	0	0			
Worcester,									
The Marchioness of				2	0	0			
Watts, J.	...	...		2	0	0			
Worthington, A. O.		...		1	1	0			
Watts, F.	...	...	...	1	1	0			

Wyles, H.	...	...	...	1	1	0
Woodward, W. H.		...		1	1	0
Warner, G. E.		...	...	1	0	0
Woodward, Hubert			...	0	10	6
Younger, W.		...	...	5	0	0
Zbrowski, Count			...	5	5	0

APPENDIX III

TOM FIRR'S RECORD

Born: Essex Kennels, Copt Hall, 12 April 1841.

Education: Local schools at Epping. As a boy he helped his father in the Essex and Puckeridge kennels and he spent a year with the South Oxfordshire, in Lord Macclesfield's employ, working in the kennels and was sometimes to be seen in the field.

Mr. Hobson's Harriers, 1859, 2nd whipper-in. Master and huntsman: George Hobson.

Cambridgeshire, 1860, 2nd whipper-in. Master: Charles Barnett. Huntsman: John Press.

Craven, 1861, 2nd whipper-in. Master: Theobold Theobold. Huntsman: Charles Berwick.

Tedworth, 1863, 2nd whipper-in. Master: Lord Ailesbury. Huntsman: George Carter.

Quorn, 1863, 2nd whipper-in. Master: S. W. Clowes. Huntsman: John Goddard.

Eglinton, 1864, 2nd whipper-in. Master: Lord Eglinton. Huntsman: George Cox.

Pytchley, 1865, 2nd whipper-in. Master and huntsman: Col. Jack Anstruther Thomson.

North Warwickshire, 1869, huntsman. Master: Richard Lant.

Quorn, 1872, huntsman. Masters: John Coupland (1870-84); Lord Manners (1884-86); William Warner and William Paget (1886-93); Lord Lonsdale (1893-98); Tommy Burns-Hartopp (1898-1905). **Retired:** February 1899. **Died:** 16 December 1902, aged 61. Buried at Quorn.

★ ★ ★

APPENDIX IV

Bibliography

Many books and periodicals have been studied during the research for this biography. Among the books, foremost is Colin Ellis's *Leicestershire and the Quorn Hunt*, for its general survey of the period. More detailed information, including reports of runs, can be obtained from the writings of Captain Pennell-Elmhirst (Brooksby) and Otho Paget (Q). The social side and alternative versions of some runs are provided by Lady Augusta Fane. W.C.A. Blew's *The Quorn Hunt and its Masters* (1899) contains only fleeting references to Tom Firr.

The Cream of Leicestershire, by Brooksby (Routledge, 1883).
The Best Season on Record, Brooksby (Routledge, 1884).
Three Great Runs, ed. Col Anstruther Thomson (Blackwood, 1889).
Riding Recollections and Turf Stories, Henry Custance (Edward Arnold, 1894).
Annals of the Warwickshire Hunt, Sir C. Mordaunt and W. Verney (S. Low, Marston, 1896).
The Essex Foxhounds, R. F. Bell and Tresham Gilbey (Vinton, 1896).
The Encyclopaedia of Sport, ed. Lord Suffolk and Berkshire (Lawrence & Bullen, 1897).
The Reminiscences of Frank Gillard, Cuthbert Bradley (Edward Arnold, 1898).
Hunting, Otho Paget (Dent, 1900).
Eighty Years' Reminiscences, J. Anstruther Thomson (Longman, Green, 1904).
Foxhunting from Shire to Shire, Cuthbert Bradley (Routledge, 1912).
Memories of the Shires, Otho Paget (Methuen, 1920).
Chit Chat, Lady Augusta Fane (Thornton Butterworth, 1926).
Memoirs of Racing and Hunting, Duke of Portland (Faber & Faber, 1935).
The History of the Althorp and Pytchley, T. Guy Paget (Collins, 1937).
Reminiscences of a Sporting Artist, Lionel Edwards (Putnam, 1947).
A Huntsman's Log Book, Isaac Bell (Eyre & Spottiswoode, 1947).
The Life of Frank Freeman, T. Guy Paget (Edgar Backus, Leicester, 1948).
A History of the Puckeridge Hunt, Michael F. Berry (Country Life, 1950).
Leicestershire and the Quorn Hunt, Colin D. B. Ellis (Backus, 1951).
The Book of the Foxhound, Daphne Moore (J. A. Allen, 1964).
The Yellow Earl, Douglas Sutherland (Cassell, 1965).

Various periodicals are mines of information, including *The Field*, *Baily's Magazine*, *Land and Water*, *The County Gentleman*, *The Loughborough Herald* and *The Leicester Chronicle and Mercury*.

★   ★   ★

INDEX

161

163